Habit Building

Your Daily Bible to Change Your Life in 7 Days, Build Your Routine and Learn the Power to Focus Your Mind on High Performance Habits

Stephen Charles Clear

circumstances will any legal responsibility or blame be held against the publisher for any reparation, damages, or monetary loss due to the information herein, either directly or indirectly.

Respective authors own all copyrights not held by the publisher.

The information herein is offered for informational purposes solely, and is universal as so. The presentation of the information is without contract or any type of guarantee assurance.

The trademarks that are used are without any consent, and the publication of the trademark is without permission or backing by the trademark owner. All trademarks and brands within this book are for clarifying purposes only and are the owned by the owners themselves, not affiliated with this document

Table of Contents

Prologue

Part 1: A Journey of Self-Exploration

    1. Self-Awareness

    2. How Did We Get Here?

    3. Do We Want to Be Here?

Part 2: The Desire to Change

    1. Motivation

    2. Willpower

    3. Relapse

Part 3: Focus on Habits

    1. Beyond Our Conscious Actions

    2. The Habit Loop

    3. Tampering with Our Habits

    4. Goal Setting

Your 7-Day Transformation Guide

Transform Your Life with Habits

Prologue

The bar in the corner of the neighborhood is a place for many things. Some go there to search for love, some have established it as their social gathering spot on weekends, and others go to escape the burdens of their everyday lives. But it's different for Adam.

Adam has been working as a bartender for over five years in that bar. For him, it is a place in which he gets to witness firsthand human stories unraveling. Adam is quite loved by all of his customers. That's not surprising; he always has the right order at the right time, and he always knows exactly what to say. In a place where everyone seems to be looking for answers, Adam appears to have them all.

Just like every other weekend, the bar went on with its routine. It's the same regular customers, each performing their usual exact patterns. If you asked him, Adam would be able to tell you what everyone in the room was doing, or was going to do.

He'd tell you about Emily who's sitting in the furthest corner, trying, but failing, to hide out of sight. Emily is certainly impressive; she can be called a genius. She's always got top grades, and she's currently preparing her masters as a medical resident in the top hospital in the country. And yet, as impressive as her brains and career are, she's struggling with a lot of insecurities. Despite her deepest desires, the pounds of fat covering her body make it impossible for her to hide in the shadows. She's a really sweet girl once you get to know her, but let's be honest, that's not what most guys try to do. Adam's guess is that her eating habits got out of control to the point she couldn't fix it anymore. It's understandable, given her academic achievements. It can be very easy to fall into bad habits of stress-eating, eating because of boredom, or eating for comfort during long hours of sitting in front of a book, studying. And yet, in that bar, Emily seems to have some peace of mind. She's able to somehow slide into the shadows, thanks to Peter.

Peter is the soul of the party. Everyone likes to be around him. No matter how dull the room is, he's able to light it up with his sense of humor. He makes friends with everyone, and he can never sit still. If he's not dancing, he's running around the tables initiating conversations. But if there's one thing you can't imagine Peter without, it's a cigarette in his hand. Whenever he finishes one, he takes no time to light the next. That would explain why he's always coughing, and why the cough just keeps on getting worse. Peter started smoking at the young age of 14, when it was a trademark of all the cool kids to be smoking. Now that he's 25, he's already outgrown that age of hanging out with the cool kids. But he can't seem to quit smoking, he's tried. He can't seem to function without the daily dose of nicotine in his blood. He needs nicotine to focus on work, and there can't be a party without smoking. Despite coughing his lungs out, he reaches out for the next cigarette every time.

The bar can be quite the party for youngsters, but that doesn't stop Michael, who's 55 years of age, from being a frequent customer. As a matter of fact, party or no party, Michael seems to always be present in the bar. It's a little bit worrisome, truth be told. No matter how early it is in the day, Michael finds his way there. From his stagger, Adam can always tell that whatever he's ordering won't be his first drink that day. He certainly seems to have a lot of time on his hands after retirement, but he seems to be wasting all his life savings on alcohol. Granted, he'd always found time for alcohol, even way before his retirement. *Being stuck in a routine job is quite boring*, he'd tell you. *What's even more boring is having your kids move out. Sucks the soul out of the house. But alcohol always makes it feel a little better, and always a little better.* Until it's too much.

The one thing that Adam wouldn't be able to explain that night is that when the doors opened, James was standing there. James. Adam hadn't seen him in like three whole years. He used to be one of the top customers, but he disappeared after his life fell apart. He used to be an alcoholic, he gained too much weight over the years, and the stench of cigarettes never left his clothes. His gambling problems got so out of hand that he lost all of his money. It was only a matter of time when he would be fired from his job and dumped by his girlfriend. This all happened five years ago. But two years later,

Adam ran into him on the street. He couldn't recognize him at all. He wore a fancy suit, had a ring on his left hand. He looked neat, wealthy, healthy, and very fit. Adam couldn't believe the transformation, it was quite a sight. But why was James back at the bar? Why did he gain all of this weight back? And most shockingly, why did he seem to have traveled five years back in time?

Working in that bar for years now, Adam has witnessed first-hand a lot of stories about all kinds of people out there. He's become so familiar with their habits, routines, behaviors, and lives that he can tell you in detail what every one of his regular customers is going to order, do, or say. After his shift is over, he can almost hear their distinct tones as they talk and interact with others. He's always been the kind of person who listened, and the type who observed the little things people did without noticing. He's also quite interested in the stories that they tell without talking. You could say he's able to read people just from the way they act. By being so good at reading people, if he could say so himself, he can predict where every one of them is going. But James had managed to shock the life out of him with his transformation once, and he managed to do the exact same thing again.

Adam spent his walk home pondering on this mystery. Before he'd realized, he was already at his doorstep taking his keys out, opening the door, and turning on the lights to an empty home. He closed the door, took off his shoes, and carried on with his nightly routine without giving it any conscious effort. He'd take a shower, pour himself some green tea, set his bedside lamp to relax, take out his book, and settle in bed. It had all become a natural routine. He'd read for twenty minutes before doing some breathing exercises, and then drink some water, turn off the lights, and sleep.

If you asked him, he'd tell you his life was peaceful and exactly how he'd want it to be. He loves being single; relationships are too disruptive for his peace of mind. He's had his own share of difficulties in life, but not anymore. The routine is comfortable, and he'd never give it up. There are some things he'd never tell you, however. Like how some nights he wishes there was someone he'd get to share the little things with. How, sometimes, some strange questions pop out of nowhere and disturb his peace of mind. How he gets the feeling he has the potential to do so much more than merely being a bartender. These are questions about his existence, and how far he wants his life to go. They bring back many memories of his previous life, when he was an aspiring young man with a lot of goals and dreams. He once believed in love, but one failed relationship after the other slowly turned him into a skeptic. As soon as these questions force themselves into his consciousness, he quickly pushes them to the back of his mind. As far as he's concerned, there's no meaning in living. He can only wait for days to pass him by, peacefully, as he watches other people and reads his precious books.

Life can be difficult, and we all have our own struggles. As life becomes more stressful, every one of us finds different coping mechanisms. Some turn to smoking; it gives them a chemical boost that makes them feel more productive. Others turn to alcohol so they can, for a very brief period of time, forget about everything and live in the moment. Others turn to food, sex, gambling, or any other distraction they can find. But as many people fall into these "bad" habits, others choose to deal with their hardships in a different, healthier way. They turn to exercise, human interaction, work, and other habits that are often described as healthy.

Those who are now struggling with bad habits didn't plan on letting them get out of control in the first place. It was a coping mechanism against stress. They completely had it under control. The guy who tried a cigarette for the first time was warned that soon enough, he wouldn't be able to stop smoking. But that was nonsense; after all, he was no loser. The girl who took out a snack every time she was bored or nervous didn't imagine that one day, weighing herself on a scale would become her biggest fear. The alcoholic doesn't want to be one, the gambler wants to stop gambling once and for all. But every time they try to put an end to their bad habits, their nature gets the better of them. No matter how strong-willed they are, no matter how many promises they make to themselves and their loved ones, they feel like they're prisoners to their actions.

It makes sense now, how James, who'd gotten his life back together, came back to the same old bar again. He'd quit drinking, overcome his nicotine and gambling addictions, got his life back on track, and become what people would describe as the most successful version of himself. But one day, as soon as he got the news of his wife's death in an accident, his life fell apart. Everything he had worked so hard to achieve seemed pointless to him, and the impact of the shock moved his legs to the old, almost-forgotten path that led to the eventful bar.

For many of us, it seems our lives are hopeless. Everything around us, from advertisements to products, from real estate to cars, from corporate to independent contractors; everything in our world today highlights, in capital, bold letters, how much we lack. Everything is telling us that we're not enough, that we don't "have" enough. We graduate from school to find ourselves buried under the tremendous weight of expectations. To be successful, you need to make enough money to get an apartment, a car, fancy clothes, luxurious gadgets, and somehow have a life at the same time. You need to find love and make it work, build a family and be happy. But the reality is, most of us aren't happy. We're just struggling to get by. And as we try to do it, everyone has a different story to tell.

The stories often recount the heart-aching struggles of an insecure young employee who lacks the confidence to ask for a raise. How overweight people keep finding comfort in food, in denial of their state, because losing all that weight just seems hopeless. How struggling adults run out of money to save, how all of their salaries seem to disappear into thin air. We find many aspiring graduates making plans to rule the world, but they hardly find the time or the opportunity to ever realize those plans. And even those who've landed the job of their dreams, after a while, feel stuck in a routine, and they struggle to focus on their work.

What do all of these people have in common? And if being the most successful, happy, and peaceful version of yourself is impossible to achieve, then how come there are hundreds of people out there who have been able to do it? Is it only a matter of time until they relapse and fail? Is it the best course of action to be just like the bartender; indifferent and waiting for his time to come?

At some point in this prologue, you must have related to a story, or at least found some comfort in knowing that you're not alone. It must also be starting to look really dark and hopeless. I'm sure you don't need any more of this darkness; if you're reading this book, it means you've come here for answers. What you'll get from this book, however, is much more than just some magical answers. I'm going to guide you through understanding yourself better, as becoming self-aware is the first step in identifying any problem you're struggling with. As you keep on reading, you'll realize how human beings are mainly controlled by a group of habits they've developed over time, and how these habits shape their life, even when they don't take notice.

You'll get to understand how both the most and least successful people are where they are right now because of the routines they've set for themselves. How, hopeless as it may seem, you have the ability to reshape your life in whichever way you set your mind to. You'll learn how to break away from bad habits once and for all, create new ones that'll stick around for the rest of your life, and set achievable goals to be the best version of yourself. And in doing so, you'll finally be able to relate to those few individuals who were able to make it, despite all odds, despite popular opinion, and despite every struggle. The best part of it all, this book gives you the latest scientific discoveries, backed with decades of research, to assert the credibility of all the strategies we'll present to you.

So prepare yourself a cup of coffee, set up your reading session, and get ready to turn your life around—for good!

Part 1: A Journey of Self-Exploration

1. Self-Awareness

Technology has surely made our lives much easier in recent decades, and yet, our fast-paced lives have gotten the better of us. Many of us believe that the most successful people are those who can perform multiple tasks at the same time. In a way, that makes a lot of sense. The more of a multitasker you are, the more you'll be able to get done, and the faster you'll achieve success.

But this theory doesn't seem to work for us very well in real life. Here we are, in the golden age of technology and multitasking, but we're less focused than ever. Achieving our goals seems impossible without letting one aspect of our lives take over the rest. We can work hard, but in return, we neglect our physical and mental health. Perhaps if we can take a moment to pause, breathe, and take it slowly for once, we can start to make sense of what's working in our life, and what is not. Maybe we'll finally realize where exactly we stand.

Before we embark on our journey, remember to take a deep breath.

Good, now we're good to go.

Did you take a deep breath? When you did, did you notice how your chest moved upwards and your stomach inwards? I'd always thought that when I take a deep breath, as my lungs get filled with air and my diaphragm pushes my stomach downwards, my abdomen would move outwards. It was an interesting discovery when one day, as I was reading about the proper ways of deep-breathing, I realized for the first time in my life that the image I had of myself when taking a deep breath was all mixed up.

Every day, we perform billions of actions without really giving them any conscious thought. Whether our abdomen moves in or out while breathing may not be significant at all, but what about all the other little things? We'll surely notice when we suddenly find ourselves in a foul mood. But where did it come from?

Why do we feel hurt, angry, depressed? What makes us feel happy, relaxed, satisfied or at peace? Why do we drink coffee first thing in the morning, or take a cigarette break in the middle of a tedious task? I can't really tell you the reason behind every emotion you feel or every action you take, but I can tell you how to find out for yourself. It all starts with becoming self-aware.

Self-awareness can be confused with self-consciousness. However, being able to understand your feelings and behaviors, in other words, being self-aware, is much different from being self-conscious. Self-consciousness can make you feel nervous when you walk into a crowd, fearing what they may think of you. It can hold you back from raising your hand to answer a question you know how to solve, just because you don't want any eyes on you. If you're having a bad hair day, you become more self-conscious about your appearance. Self-consciousness is all about concentrating on what "others" think of you, and in that sense, it affects how you see yourself. Self-awareness is the complete opposite.

When you delve deep into your own thoughts, feelings, and actions; when you start noticing the patterns you go through every time a situation is repeated, you take the first steps of your self-awareness journey. It helps you understand yourself better—what you're good at and what has more room for improvement; how your feelings affect your actions; how your small unconscious habits have a big impact on your success in life. According to psychologists, there's one trait that all highly successful people have in common. Can you guess what that trait is? That's right, it's that they're all extremely self-aware.

Self-awareness is considered to be the cornerstone of emotional and social intelligence, as well as achieving whatever you set your mind to achieve. However, if becoming self-aware was as easy as pointing it out, most of us wouldn't be struggling where we are right now. So why is it so difficult to develop? And how do you become self-aware?

Let's do a quick experiment.

In one sentence, describe yourself in your home. Then describe yourself in one sentence at work, and in another sentence in a social situation, while you're at a party, the gym, or the club.

Next, ask one person in each of the previous settings to describe your personality. You can ask a member of your family, a co-worker, and a close friend or an acquaintance.

You'll end up with a lot of insight after this exercise, and we'll break it down in just a second. But the first thing you need to remember is to receive feedback from others objectively. Don't get angry, stressed, confused, or start overthinking about their descriptions of you if that's not how you see yourself. In fact, getting different opinions about you is the whole point of this exercise.

So the first thing you'll notice about the feedback is that people in different settings have varying descriptions of you. That's expected, as your family sees you in different situations than your coworkers do. Depending on the time and place, you will show different aspects of your personality. Is that a bad thing? Not at all. As human beings, we are widely diverse, and our personalities and characteristics are quite complicated. Having a serious face all the time at home won't establish strong family bonds, and joking around all the time at work will mask your professional side. That's why your family can describe you as "warm and loving," your coworkers as "professional," and your friends as "outgoing and fun to hang out with." Each of them describes the person that they see in certain controlled situations. But how did you describe yourself in those settings?

More often than not, we have these "standards" of ourselves, and accordingly, we frame images of how we see ourselves. These standards and principles vary a lot based on our upbringing, experiences, values, and beliefs. A workaholic can have an image of themselves as hard-working, professional, ambitious, and a know-it-all. But as they shift all of their focus to work, their family and friends can describe them as "absent, lonely, and mysterious". A kind-hearted person can think of themselves as a loving and caring friend, but others would describe them as "emotional and dramatic." So who is right and who is wrong? What is good and what is bad?

As a matter of fact, when it comes to people, there's no such thing as right and wrong, or good and bad. Becoming self-aware has nothing to do with labeling people.

Self-awareness is the key to understanding why we think, feel, and act the way we do. Once we understand the complex workings of our minds, once we're able to break down our thoughts and emotions, we'll be able to either embrace who we are or change what we don't like about ourselves. That's why the first step to becoming self-aware is comparing the image we have of ourselves to how others see us through different perspectives.

So tell me, how different were the answers you received compared to how you've described yourself? The closer the answer, the more self-aware you are. It doesn't mean that a completely irrelevant answer shows that you're wrong about yourself or that they're wrong about you. It just means that you weren't quite aware of yourself and the impression you leave on those around you. That can be the result of being unable to express yourself clearly, or not taking as much notice of your surroundings as you thought you did. It also shows how most of our interactions with each other can be shallow and superficial, only lasting the duration of the point of contact. Another point to pay attention to in this scenario is that people will often build their own judgments and perceptions about you, based on their own backgrounds. This can say a lot about their personalities and characters as well. But anyway, back to our self-awareness lesson.

What makes others' feedback so important is that it gets us out of the bubble we've created for ourselves. It shocks us to hear negative feedback when someone points out our flaws. Usually, our reaction is that of denial, and sometimes justified excuses. But do we ever stop at that negative feedback and examine its origins? Do you, in fact, sometimes get angry about the smallest things? Do you react strongly to what makes you feel sad or hurt? If you're having a bad day at home, do you carry that energy into your work environment and spend the day looking all sour? The feedback from third parties is important because it provides us with an image of ourselves, even when we're too immersed in our inner environment to notice how we convey these conflicts to the outside world. It gives us a raw, honest assessment of our weaknesses and flaws, but it also helps us objectively explore our strengths and passions.

Knowing where we stand in life is critical to correctly assess ourselves and our lives, and in turn have a solid base in making life-changing decisions. We've discussed how critical self-awareness is to being successful, but how exactly do we cultivate it?

We'll break down self-awareness into three levels. The first level is understanding our inner environment: the emotions we feel, what we think of our passions, strengths, and weaknesses, and how connected to the present moment we are. The second level is our outer self-awareness, which is how aware we are of what others think of us. The third level is the connection between our emotions and how we act based on what we're feeling.

Inner Self-Awareness: Emotional Intelligence

It can sound pretty easy, but actually only a limited number of people really know themselves. Even less are those who've become friends with themselves.

There are many exercises to become more self-aware, but let's start with a simple—and severely underestimated—exercise: meditation. Some start their morning routine with meditation, others like to end their day with it. Don't think too much about when to perform this exercise, just get started and then you'll find its place in your routine.

Find a quiet and relaxing setting, be it in front of a garden, in an air-conditioned room with the lights dimmed down, or even on your vacation in front of the sea. What are you feeling right now? List three feelings you've experienced in the previous 24 hours. Were you able to name the emotions you've felt?

There's a popular strategy in Neuro-Linguistic Programming that's known to really help people deal with feelings. It's called "naming your emotions," and it's something that emotionally-intelligent people know how to use very well. It may seem like a very simple thing to do, but its effects are huge. Let's do a quick exercise to see how we normally react, and compare it to the effects of emotional intelligence on our behavior.

The first emotions that come to our mind are usually the final emotions that we express. We can easily express anger, sadness, and happiness. We can start with anger; list a couple of situations in which you've felt angry. Now, break them down. Why did you feel angry in each situation? Try to reflect on your emotions in a broader sense. What about when you felt happy or sad? After pinning down the situation, identifying the emotion and the reason behind it, think of alternative ways you could have expressed your feelings. Afterward comes three important questions: Do you like the way you reacted? Why did you react that way? Why didn't you express it differently?

Here's an example of how to break down this exercise:

Situation: I shouted at my kids.

Emotion: Angry.

Reason: They were making a mess in the living room, and they were going around making loud noises early in the morning.

Alternative scenario #1: Call them together for a different game that requires less noise.

Alternative scenario #2: Tell them you'll treat them to hot chocolate if they keep their voices down.

Alternative scenario #3: Ask them to lower their voices because you have a bad headache. "And look at all the mess you're making! Mom will be furious."

Alternative scenario #X: There really are many alternative scenarios you can think of, but let's keep it at 3.

And the main questions now are:

Do you like the way you reacted?

Of course not, no one feels good after shouting at their kids.

Why did you react that way? Before resorting to the same reason you've just given a while ago, try to express it based on your own inner experience. Instead of describing how *others* made you react the way you did, try to describe why *you* reacted that way. Here's the difference between both answers:

"They were making a mess in the living room, and they were going around making loud noises early in the morning."

"I woke up with a bad headache and couldn't tolerate loud noises in the morning. The headache made me feel on the edge, so my first reaction was to get angry about the noise, which made me shout at the kids."

Why didn't you express your anger differently? Sometimes we run short of answers to such a question. It just happened on the spur of the moment, you didn't plan on shouting. But right there, you just got your answer.

"I didn't think about it before I reacted. I let my emotions—which resulted from my disturbed inner environment—take over."

Getting to know your inner environment and how it works makes it easier for you to identify your emotions and explain your actions. In the previous example, becoming self-aware can help you change a certain behavior you don't like. But it can also help you deal with a depressive episode, ease your anxiety, define what makes you happy, achieve more happiness, and even know what drives your success and how to maintain it.

But let's take it one step at a time. Today, you've taken a great first step toward identifying an emotion, digging deep into it, defining how that emotion influenced your actions, and you've even expressed your disapproval of the original action. Well done!

Outer Self-Awareness: Social Intelligence

Using the same example, we'll tackle the situation from a different perspective. How do you think the kids felt after their father shouted at them, so early in the morning, when they were just having some harmless fun on their weekend?

Without giving it much—or any—thought, their father just bawled them out. They *forced* him to do so, he'd justify. However, the impact of this behavior may stay on the children's minds for years. If it's a common occurrence, they can grow up scared of their father. Some may feel insecure in their own homes, which can terribly affect their sense of self-worth. They might grow up living in fear, not being able to trust or fully love their father. The case can be much more severe if, in anger, the parents resort to more violent measures.

Did the father intend to cause all of this? He just wanted some peace in the morning. But when he reacted right away, when he let his emotions lead the way to an uncontrolled expression of anger, he caused much more damage than he would ever have meant to.

Starting to realize the impact of your presence and actions on your surroundings helps you build a more accurate image of yourself. The father would've described himself as a doting, loving parent who works tirelessly to provide for his family. But the little children who only understand reality based on their own limited experience won't appreciate the effort their father exerts for their sake just yet. So the father—the adult—needs to ask himself a question after coming to this realization: is this how he wants his kids to think of him while growing up? If not, then he needs to do something about his behavior.

The good (and bad) thing is that we are creatures of habit. Years of repeating the same action will make it highly probable that we repeat our behavioral mistakes again and again. But once we realize how we're driven by our habits, as well as our internal and external environments, we'll have a much bigger chance at changing what we don't like in our behavior, and fortifying our "good" behavior.

In the same scenario breakdown, outer self-awareness—or as some would call it, "social intelligence"—can be extended to all of your environments. Knowing the workings of your inner environment is important, but without becoming aware of your surroundings, you'll still remain in a somewhat bigger bubble. It all depends on your personality, nature, and what you want to achieve. When a person finds the balance they need between their inner and outer environments, they can achieve anything.

There are centuries-old studies that have tackled the two social natures of people: introverts and extroverts. Even modern personality tests are based on evaluating this nature, and depending on the results, they recommend the most suitable jobs for people according to their personalities.

Introverts are often described as "shy," as they're easily shadowed by the existence of active and outgoing extroverts. Extroverts find little difficulty in speaking up, and they effortlessly become the soul of the party. After all, they're able to recharge their energy through social interactions. On the other hand, introverts feel drained by social interactions. They'd rather keep to themselves in their quiet, peaceful, and controlled environments. When chaos enters their world, like being in a party, they feel like their souls are disturbed. They need their alone time to recharge. But if we are defined by our natures, if we can't change our behavior because "that's just who we are," then how come there's a third classification of people, known as ambiverts?

Ambiverts are those who have found a balance between being an introvert and an extrovert. They like the peace and calmness of their alone time, but they're able to enjoy meeting up and going out with other people. Even though they're mostly introverts who need to spend some time alone to recharge, they can still function in various environments and maintain healthy social relationships. So what's their secret?

To put it simply, their secret is that they've found a balance through understanding their nature and what they need. They provide themselves with time to recharge and focus on themselves, while they also understand how relationships, if healthy, can add a lot of positive energy into their lives. So they consciously choose where to place their spare energy. They'll still feel drained in awkward social occasions, but they have enough emotional and social intelligence to set up the environments they need to stay healthy.

Social intelligence comes in handy, especially in the workplace. Being introverts by nature, ambiverts will be able to excel at tasks that they perform alone, needing little communication. But our fast-paced lives make it critical for any employee to be a team player. Does this mean there's no place for introverts in the work environments of today? Not at all. This fact only serves to stress how important it is for us to be socially aware, to understand our outer self-awareness and to find the balance between our internal and external environments.

The reason why high social intelligence matters so much in professional life is that a healthy work environment is one of the leading causes of success. When employees are able to communicate with one another clearly, understand each other, and accept their differences, they'll be able to focus on their tasks much better. A lot of energy goes to waste due to insignificant issues, which often only result from miscommunication. A socially intelligent person will know how to express their thoughts clearly to avoid miscommunication, and realize if a coworker is not in their best mood on a certain day, so they'll perhaps go easy on them that day. Even better, offering help or a listening ear will strengthen the bond between the two of them. Understanding coworkers means a healthier work culture, which in turn makes work more efficient, cuts down on time-wasting issues and makes room for employees to actually feel good at work. The whole workplace is affected, and everybody wins.

The Bridge Between Inner & Outer Environments

One of my all-time favorite quotes is from Viktor E. Frankl, where he explains:

"Between stimulus and response, there is a space. In that space is our power to choose our response. In our response lies our growth and our freedom."

At times when our emotions are overwhelming and our minds aren't thinking straight, taking a moment to pause and think before we react can have life-changing results. It might seem impossible in the heat of the moment, but that's where emotional conditioning comes into play.

After learning how to reflect on our inner selves, identify our emotions and our unconditioned first reactions, as well as realizing our impact on the outer environment and its impact on us, we'll have the main tools for developing our self-awareness. Now comes the part where we learn how to link them all together in a way that will be unique for every one of us. After all, we're all searching for the perfect balance within ourselves, and no two human beings are ever identical.

I wish I could tell you there's a magical button you can press to build this link; there's not. But I'll tell you the next best thing, which is the fact that the more you practice your self-awareness, the more naturally you will start to notice—and change—everything. Building this bridge takes a lot of conscious effort to reprogram how you've been conditioned to think, feel, and act. It's the collective effort you put into your meditation each day, the feedback you get from those around you, and your reflection on whether you've acted the way you really wanted to.

In this part of developing self-awareness, I'll give you one more exercise. Focus on one emotion you want to control better. Some of the most toxic emotions that can be really difficult to shake off once they possess us are anger, anxiety, and sadness. Focus on the emotion that gives you the most trouble. Keep a journal nearby, and for the duration of one day, write down every time you've felt that emotion. Write it down in a way similar to the exercise we've done a while ago:

Emotion: Identify the emotion.

External reason: What happened in your external environment that made you feel that emotion?

Internal reason: Dig a bit deeper and figure out the reason why you've felt that way, and not any other way.

Your reaction: How did you react?

Alternative scenarios: Pick 3 different scenarios that could've played out instead of the original outcome.

Then choose one alternative scenario, and decide that the next time you're faced with a similar situation, that's how you're going to react. Here's a heads-up: there's a very high possibility that you'll forget to react differently on the spur of the moment. Don't feel discouraged, that's completely natural and expected. The whole point of this exercise, however, is to keep trying until you make it. Make a record of every failed trial in your journal, and when you finally succeed, tell me... how many times did it take you to make it?

Where Do We Stand?

I think it's time for us to answer one of our main questions: *"Where do we stand?"*

We'll do one more exercise.

We'll start this exercise in our meditation settings once again, keeping our spirits relaxed and peaceful. This time, I'll guide you while you reflect back on different aspects of your life.

The aspects of human life are diverse, and that's how beautifully complicated human beings are. Especially in an age where everyone is running marathons—figuratively speaking—we find ourselves involved in many environments. Everyone has their own priorities and interests, but somewhere along the line, we all intersect at one place or another.

What are your interests and priorities in life? For the sake of categorizing the aspects and making them easier to analyze, we'll divide them into:

Family

Career

Social life

Physical life

Spiritual life

Material life

Where do you stand in each of these categories? Describe where you are in detail, and try as much as you can to mention the positive and negative aspects of your situation.

Here's an example:

Family:

"I wish I could find a partner, but I don't think I'm good enough for anyone. I'd be willing to go the extra mile for the right person!"

Or

"I have a family, but I never find the time to enjoy together because I'm very stressed at work."

Career:

"I'm working at a company right now. I keep looking for jobs but it feels like I'll never be satisfied or reach financial stability."

Or

"There are a lot of problems at work, and I have difficulty communicating with my coworkers or expressing myself properly to my boss... but I'm still trying."

Social Life:

"I have no social life; I'm so focused on my family and work that I don't have any time for socializing."

Or

"I can go out of my way for my friends, but I don't feel they'd do the same for me."

Physical Life:

"I'd rather not pass anywhere near the scale."

Or

"I smoke too many cigarettes a day, I feel tired all the time... I wish I could go to the gym and start taking care of my health a bit more."

Spiritual Life:

"I don't feel peaceful and relaxed, mostly I'm just anxious, angry, or depressed."

Material Life:

"I wish I could buy a car."

Or

"I'm always short of money and I can't save up."

Let's recap what we've discussed so far. We've gone through inner self-awareness, which can also be called emotional intelligence. This skill helps us realize the deeper workings of our emotions and how they influence our behavior. We've learned from discussing outer self-awareness, aka social intelligence, how our behavior affects our environment, and how our external environment influences our feelings at the same time. *Realizing* how everything works was the first step. As any psychologist would tell you, "a problem well-stated is a problem half-solved."

Then, we've utilized our self-awareness knowledge to define where we stand in our lives. What makes us happy, sad, angry, dissatisfied, or even satisfied? We've learned how to notice the way we react in any given situation, and how our actions influence our emotions and our external environments.

Next comes the part where you decide which parts of your life you want to change.

2. How Did We Get Here?

So far, you've listed the issues you're not satisfied with in your life. Next step is to use what you've learned from the self-awareness exercises to analyze why you're stuck where you are right now. For the previous answers, the analysis can go as follows:

Family:

Situation: *I can't find a partner, and I don't believe I'm worthy of love.*

Analysis: *I wish I could find a partner, but I don't think I'm good enough for anyone, because I think I'm boring, overweight, or not good-looking enough. I'd be willing to go the extra mile for the right person.*

How you got here: *I'm scared of trying new things, or generally I'm scared of putting myself out there. I'm always worried about what others think of me; I can feel them staring and making fun of me everywhere I go. I'm not one* of the "cool" kids, I'm quiet and I keep to myself most of the time. If I stay in my own little world, no one can harm me.

Or

Situation: *I give all my energy to work and I'm wasting the chance to watch my children grow up.*

Analysis: *I have a family, but I never find the time to enjoy together because I'm very stressed at work. I put a lot of stress on myself because I need to work hard to prove myself. If I don't work overtime and burn the candle at both ends, I feel I'll never achieve what I want in my career! But that affects my family, as I'm almost always absent.*

How you got here: *I believe that having a successful career is directly related to how much effort I put into it. I'm not the smartest guy in the room, and I'm not as naturally talented or skilled as others. So I compensate what I feel I'm lacking by giving 150% of my energy to work, even if that means being absent from my family's life.*

Career:

Situation: *I keep overthinking, I lack motivation, and I have no idea what I'm doing with my life.*

Analysis: *I'm working at a company right now. I keep looking for jobs but it feels like I'll never be satisfied or reach financial stability. Even though I'm working, my mind is always wandering to what I don't have, and what I can't do.*

How you got here: *I'm not sure what exactly I want to do in life, I've been wandering for a very long time, applying for a job after another, but I don't feel focused or motivated at any job. I just go with the flow. People keep talking to me about goals and achievements in life, but I'm just trying to figure out what to have for breakfast the next day. I'm confused and lost, so I just keep searching.*

Or

Situation: *Work is good but working with people is stressful. I find it difficult to communicate with people or work in a team.*

Analysis: *There are a lot of problems at work, and I have difficulty communicating with my coworkers or expressing myself properly to my boss... but I'm still trying. I like taking tasks and working on them, but I can't focus in the middle of a crowd. Sometimes I can see solutions clearly but I'm afraid of speaking my mind, in case my idea was stupid. I see many problems in the work environment, but I'm worried that if I mention them to my boss, my colleagues will get angry with me for selling them out. Dealing with human beings is so distressing; you never know how they'll react.*

How you got here: *Ever since I was young, I was silent most of the time. I usually don't have a particular opinion to share, but have felt pressured to form opinions so others would approve of me. But people always have different opinions, if I chose the wrong one I would offend someone. So I chose to be silent, to avoid any conflict. But now people think of me as ignorant, and I still feel pressured to fit in and, somehow, manage to not annoy anyone.*

Social Life:

Situation: *I overwork and leave no time for social relationships.*

Analysis: *I have no social life, I'm so focused on my family and work that I don't have any time for socializing. I have my priorities; socializing and making friends aren't as important to me as my other goals. But sometimes I just wish I had a friend to share some good times with.*

How you got here: *I always push people away, in the end, it never works anyway. I've realized that work is what matters; the more successful I'll become the less I'll need people to fill the void. Work will never let me down, I just need to keep working, and eventually I'll find my place.*

Or

Situation: *I feel insecure, taken for granted, and left behind.*

Analysis: *I can go out of my way for my friends, but I don't feel they'd do the same for me. I can't shake off the feeling that I'm always the second option and someone everyone takes me for granted. I feel like I have to put a lot of effort into my friendships, but everyone else seems to look out for themselves.*

How you got here: *I don't really make time for myself. I can give unconditionally and put others before myself. I'm always there, and I'll never say no, so I'm expected to always stay there. To be honest, I always build my sense of self-esteem on what I do for others, so I keep neglecting myself in the process.*

Physical Life:

Situation: *I've gained so much weight and I can't lose it.*

Analysis: *I'd rather not pass anywhere near the scale. I'm not sure how it got so bad, but I've gained so much weight that it's gotten out of control now. It's terrifying to think about it, so I* *just avoid the scale and thinking about my weight altogether. It's much easier that way.*

How you got here: *I found comfort in eating; it's always made me feel better. When I was bored, I'd just find myself walking over to the kitchen to snack on anything I found. Eventually, that became a habit, and I could hardly resist temptation when it came to food.*

Or

Situation: *My smoking habits have gotten out of control.*

Analysis: *I smoke too many cigarettes a day, I feel tired all the time... I wish I could go to the gym and start taking care of my health a bit more.*

How you got here: *At first, I started smoking although everyone told me how addictive it was going to get. I gave little thought to what they said, I told myself I'd just stop whenever I wanted to. Eventually, I stopped going to the gym or working out, my health kept deteriorating, but I still can't stop. When I wake* up every day, before I know it, I'm smoking a cigarette.

Spiritual Life:

Situation: *My anxiety and restlessness are controlling every aspect of my life.*

Analysis: *I don't feel peaceful and relaxed, mostly I'm just anxious, angry, or depressed. I keep thinking of worst-case scenarios, and even in my free time, I'm waiting for the worst to happen. Everyone around me keeps telling me how "negative" I am and that it's annoying. But I can't help it, it's who I am!*

How you got here: *I've been this way for as long as I can remember. I've noticed at a very young age that whenever something good happens, something bad follows. Sometimes the bad even ruins the good completely. It's scary to have hopes or experience joy, because it can easily be snatched away from your hands. It's better to expect the worst; that way, I'll be less disappointed.*

Material Life:

Situation: *I don't make enough money.*

Analysis: *I wish I could buy a car. I wish I had enough money to pamper myself every now and then. I'm not asking to be fancy rich; I just want to be able to satisfy my basic needs and give myself a good treat every once in a while.*

How you got here: *I'm always short of money and I can't save up. My salary melts away in the blink of an eye, and I can't put any of it aside. I indulge in little cravings every now and then, I often order fast food at work because it's easy and quick. I might go to the movies, but usually I'm content with my Netflix subscription. Come to think of it, I waste a lot of money on my everyday routine, but I never notice!*

The focus of this exercise is to point out what we're dissatisfied with across different aspects of our lives, then analyze our situation, and delve deep into ourselves to identify the unconscious patterns of thoughts, feelings, and behaviors that got us stuck where we are. Once we become aware of what's going wrong in our lives, we're going to list our toxic self-talk, our negative emotions, and our escapist actions, then finally reach a really important answer. What's keeping us stuck in place? Why are we dissatisfied with our reality?

3. Do We Want to Be Here?

If you're reading this book, then chances are you're looking for ways to turn your life around. You might be having difficulty focusing on work, finding a stable relationship, saving money, or achieving your goals. You might be trying to find a way to increase your self-esteem, success, and social skills. You probably aren't in a very good place right now, so, of course, there are a lot of things you're dissatisfied with. But what *exactly* are they?

After our last exercises on *"Where do we stand?"* and *"How did we get here?"* you should now be getting some answers. Before, you'd feel generally frustrated, anxious, angry, or just *not good*, but now you've learned how to identify your situation in every aspect of your life. So you're ready for my next question: Do you want to be here?

In almost all environments, we'll find that there's both good and bad. Sometimes we focus so much on the bad that we overlook the little things that *are* working. Identifying the bad is great, because that's how we'll be able to change it. But overlooking the good can make life seem dark and hopeless. That's why, before you reply to my question, let me take you on a tour through our minds, finding out how our self-talk, patterns of thought, and the way we evaluate our satisfaction can all play big parts in our dissatisfaction.

Here are the top reasons why we may be dissatisfied with our reality:

We focus on what we don't have.

It seems to be a persistent part of human nature to keep running after what we don't have. We strive for the perfect job, and when we get it, we keep waiting for a raise. We buy a car, then want the next state-of-the-art model that just hit the market. We start with our basic needs of shelter, safety, financial stability, and self-accomplishment, but somewhere along the line, we stop trying to get things because we need them, and we run after things we want. Most of us measure their success and happiness in relation to how much they have in the material world.

While pursuing success and letting it show in what you can afford is, indeed, a good achievement, problems emerge when we make what we have—or don't have—our only measure of success, and in turn, happiness. We think we'll never be happy unless we have what everyone else has, and that's a great mistake.

If having more meant more happiness, then how come we keep hearing stories of billionaires committing suicide? Why aren't they happy? Happiness is an internal state of mind, and its absence can't be filled with physical objects. Whenever we focus on what we don't have—or even worse, when we keep comparing our lives to others'—we lose focus on what really matters. What do we really want? Not because others have it, and not because we're supposed to have it, but what would we, deep down in our souls, love to have?

We have unrealistic expectations.

Losing weight isn't impossible; there are thousands of stories of extremely overweight people who were able to pull it off. But if one of them went to their dietitian and told them: "*I want to lose a hundred pounds in two weeks,"* what do you think their dietitian would say?

That's impossible.

Expecting you'll be able to run a marathon after a week of training at the gym is just as unrealistic as buying a car after getting your very first paycheck. When we set goals for ourselves that are impossible to achieve right away, we sign ourselves up for failure. If we fail at the first attempt, finding the will and motivation to start over for the second time becomes much more difficult; we start to lose hope. We become dissatisfied.

Meanwhile, if we take it slow, we'll surely make it. So next time you feel impatient about something and you want it to happen right away, try and remind yourself to have some patience.

We love to procrastinate.

Ah, the elephant in the room. Most of us wouldn't describe themselves as losers. In fact, many of the smartest people I know are lazy—they're so overconfident about their abilities and natural talent that they believe they can do anything. And yet, they still struggle in real life just like the rest of us.

Others may have a lot of self-doubt and uncertainty, so they keep procrastinating to postpone the inevitable as much as they can. They'll only get to the task when they absolutely, inescapably *need* to do it. They're scared of failure, so they'd just rather not think about it.

But where has procrastination gotten us? Very much left behind.

We found some kind of comfort zone.

Finding a comfort zone certainly helps with procrastination. If we're all safe in our tiny little bubble, nothing can affect our peace of mind.

But the fault in this pattern of thought is that this peace is often only an illusion. We *think* we're peaceful, we *think* we're safe, but in all honesty, we're only running away from reality. We're trying to avoid facing real life, whether it's the struggle to find a job, the challenges in keeping a healthy relationship, or the harsh reality that we'll need to be uncomfortable for a while until we build a better reality for ourselves.

We let escapism and distractions take control.

Staying in our comfort zone is so easy when we have any kind of distraction to escape into. If there's an abundance in one thing in this age of technology, it's the numerous forms of escapism that are at our fingertips.

Escapism can take form in any activity, from watching TV shows and movies, to deciding to sleep all day long. Worse forms of escapism are addicting activities such as seeking alcohol, drugs, sex, and self-abuse to escape reality. What does doing drugs and watching movies all day have in common? They're both means of distraction the person resorts to, in order to avoid dealing with whatever is out of their bubble. Once distraction takes the wheel, we feel secluded and safe. But once again, we're only creating a delusion for our brief peace of mind— at a costly price for our future.

We worry and overthink without taking any action.

Feeling stressed is a natural reaction to the pressure life is putting on you, but spending all of your time worrying instead of doing anything about it is a sure way to fail and feel dissatisfied. Tell me, what have you ever gotten out of worrying? Has it solved anything? Have you ever felt better after listing all of the worst-case scenarios that can unfold in your life? Has worrying about whether or not you'll get the job made the interview go smoother? Have any of the nights you've spent worrying that your wife may be cheating on you—or that one day she might—made your relationship any stronger?

Worrying only serves to strip the peace away from your current moment, without changing the future outcome. What's bound to happen is going to happen, and you'll deal with it when it does. And yes, I know it's much easier said than done, but isn't this the whole point of what we're doing? Instead of worrying about what might happen, decide that next time you'll think about what could actually go right.

We complain.

Just as much as we love procrastination, we love complaining. Complaining about our misfortunes gives us a sense of justification for not doing anything. After all, it's out of our hands. We complain about how unfair life is, how our boss favors a certain coworker over us, or how other people treat us. We complain about every single thing we're unhappy with.

All of this complaining serves as an outlet for our anger, sadness, anxiety, and dissatisfaction. Every time we give full vent to these emotions, we somehow feel better. That's because we channel some of the negative energy into complaining and we feel less burdened by it. We feel justified. But at the end of the day, we don't get anything solved. We wake up the next day and restart our complaining routine.

How about, instead of complaining about what's going wrong, you thought of it differently? Instead of believing you're the victim in your own story, you could wake up in the morning, stand in front of the mirror, and tell yourself that you're in control of your story. You're the one who gets to draw the picture, you're the one who'll choose the colors and form the image you'd like to see on whichever canvas you were served.

We have no idea what we really want.

Complaining about life is easy, procrastination comes naturally, comparing ourselves to others helps us prove how unfair life is, but these mechanisms can stem from a deeper reason. What do we really want in life?

What do we desire? What are our goals and aspirations? What makes us happy, peaceful or relaxed? If we have no idea what we want or where we want to go, how on earth are we supposed to build a life that we love? Having no idea what works for us will only keep us walking in a haze, unfocused, pursuing whatever others are pursuing for a false sense of achievement. And without the right motives or beliefs, we'll often quit midway through our journey, when it gets too tough.

After we monitor our self-talk and figure out what's keeping us from being truly happy, we can revisit our question. Do we want to be here?

What exactly don't you like about being here? The father from our previous exercises may realize after a lot of reflection that he doesn't want to be the angry father in the eyes of his children as they grow up. Someone who is overweight doesn't want to feel judged by their appearance, they want to feel attractive. The shy girl wants to be able to express her opinion out loud, and the high-school boy doesn't really want to be fail in school; he just feels that no matter what he does, he's no good academically.

Not everybody who's going through a similar situation is necessarily as bothered by it as the next person. Someone can be failing in school but not even care about it: perhaps they've found their skills and talent appreciated elsewhere so they just dropped out. An introvert might not be troubled at all by their lack of social activities. Our dissatisfaction with some aspects of our lives is ours to deal with, so the first thing we need to decide before announcing our despair is: if we change this aspect, are we doing it for ourselves? Or do we want to change it just to fit in the society? Will that really make us happy?

Once you reach your answers, you'll need to have some courage to figure out what makes you dissatisfied. It's always easy to point out our circumstances and blame our misfortune on the universe, but how on earth would you be able to *change* your reality if you think you have no power over it? It's going to take a lot of courage from you to be as brutally honest as you can be with yourself to assess your situation objectively and point out exactly the reasons that keep you stuck in place.

Once you reach your answers, you'll find a little bit of peace mixed with an uneasy feeling. It'll feel like it's going to take a lot to change your reality, and that's why you've been procrastinating it. But once you know, you know; there's no turning back. Now is the time to turn your life around, and I'll be walking by your side to guide you every step of the way.

Self-Exploration Worksheet

Inner and Outer Self-Awareness Exercises

Situation #1:

Emotion:

External reason:

Internal reason:

Alternative scenario #1:

Alternative scenario #2:

Alternative scenario #3:

Do you like the way you've reacted?

Why did you react that way?

Why didn't you express your feelings differently?

How did your reaction affect your external environment?

Situation #2:

Emotion:

External reason:

Internal reason:

Alternative scenario #1:

Alternative scenario #2:

Alternative scenario #3:

Do you like the way you've reacted?

Why did you react that way?

Why didn't you express your feelings differently?

How did your reaction affect your external environment?

Situation #3:

Emotion:

External reason:

Internal reason:

Alternative scenario #1:

Alternative scenario #2:

Alternative scenario #3:

Do you like the way you've reacted?

Why did you react that way?

Why didn't you express your feelings differently?

How did your reaction affect your external environment?

Situation #4:

Emotion:

External reason:

Internal reason:

Alternative scenario #1:

Alternative scenario #2:

Alternative scenario #3:

Do you like the way you've reacted?

Why did you react that way?

Why didn't you express your feelings differently?

How did your reaction affect your external environment?

Situation #5:

Emotion:

External reason:

Internal reason:

Alternative scenario #1:

Alternative scenario #2:   '

Alternative scenario #3:

Do you like the way you've reacted?

Why did you react that way?

Why didn't you express your feelings differently?

How did your reaction affect your external environment?

How Did You Get Here?

Situation #1:

Analysis:

How did you get here?

Situation #2:

Analysis:

How did you get here?

Situation #3:

Analysis:

How did you get here?

Situation #4:

Analysis:

How did you get here?

Situation #5:

Analysis:

How did you get here?

Part 2: The Desire to Change

We've established that we're dissatisfied with where we are, and we're willing to change what we don't like about our lives. But how do we do that? If you ask a successful person about what drives their success, you'll get many different answers depending on who you're asking. But judging by my own circle of family, friends, and coworkers, there were two answers in particular that I've received a lot: motivation and/or willpower. Those are, indeed, strong aids. It's said that where there's a will, there's a way, and that people can accomplish even the most difficult tasks if given the right motivation. So how exactly do these two secret ingredients work?

1. Motivation

What makes us do what we do? Why do we feel excited to fulfill a certain task, but another task just feels so heavy?

Psychologists have been studying motivation and where it comes from for decades, and if you do some research, you'll find different schools of thoughts, definitions, and strategies.

While the old school focused on defining motivation from a philosophical point of view, the new school focused more on how to benefit from understanding motivation to implement it in real life. The two schools can thus be divided into *content* (theory-based definitions) and *process* (strategies on how to become motivated.) The content theories give greater insight from an academic point of view, while the process strategies provide more results in practical life.

Content Theories

There are four content theories, and they revolve around analyzing **what** motivates people.

1. Maslow's Hierarchy of Needs

This is the most common and widely-known theory for what motivation is. Most of us would recognize it as the pyramid of needs, where humans find motivation in satisfying the basic needs found at the bottom of the pyramid first, and once those needs are satisfied, they become motivated to satisfy the next level.

The pyramid consists of five levels:

Physiological needs: These are the basic needs of any human; clean water, shelter, food, and sleep.

Safety and security: Long ago, this need enlisted making it through the day without getting killed while hunting, but today it revolves around financial stability, a safe place to live, and being well and healthy.

Belongingness and love: Once the previous needs are met, the human starts looking for stable relationships with family, friends, and lovers.

Self-esteem: Next comes the social standing of the individual; how they're viewed by others, how they view themselves, and how to be a reputable member of society.

Self-actualization: This is where individuals venture out to achieve their potential to the fullest. As Maslow says in this part: "What humans can be, they must be."

2. Alderfer's ERG Theory

Alderfer took an approach similar to Maslow's, but he divided motivation into three categories instead of five. He believed that humans have three needs that motivate them:

Existence: The need for physiological and physical safety measures.

Relatedness: The need for stable relationships, the feeling of belonging somewhere, and recognition in the society.

Growth: The motivation to pursue self-development, self-actualization, and self-esteem.

What makes Alderfer's ERG theory different from Maslow's, however, is his idea that while an individual is usually motivated to satisfy the unmet basic needs first, before moving to the other needs, sometimes they may move down the ladder to satisfy a lower need that's not met anymore. When higher needs are satisfied, they become more important for the individual to maintain. When a lower need that was once satisfied but isn't anymore, it takes more effort and energy to fulfill it once again.

This theory may be considered more down-to-earth because, for instance, if you find a financially satisfying job but end up losing it, the once-satisfied physical safety is no more. Meeting a certain need at some point in our lives doesn't necessarily make it permanent. So we go back and try to have it once more, but our second trial often proves to be much harder than the first.

3. McClelland's Achievement Motivation

While both Maslow and Alderfer identified motivation based on our unmet needs, McClelland focused on creating those needs and developing them. He classified our motivators into three categories:

Achievement: Where an individual is motivated to complete a task to show competency or achieve mastery.

Affiliation: Where a longing for love, relatedness, and belongingness motivates the person.

Power: Where the individual strives to take control, whether over his own work or the work of others.

This theory is also called the Learned Needs Theory. It suggests that while every one of us has those three motivators, only one motivator drives the behavior of a certain individual at any given time. Two employees can be working at the same company, under the same circumstances, and on the same task, but one will be motivated by their sense of achievement, and the other for the feeling of power.

4. Herzberg's Two-Factor Theory

Herzberg argued that there are two factors that drive motivation in the workplace: *motivating factors*, which are responsible for feelings of satisfaction; and *hygiene factors*, which are responsible for dissatisfaction. He explained that satisfaction and dissatisfaction aren't opposites, but rather, no satisfaction is the opposite of being satisfied.

The motivating factors are related to doing the job itself. Here, the greatest variables of your work satisfaction are your own personal growth, development, recognition, responsibility, and achievement. Hygiene factors involve everything that comes with this work, such as the team culture, salary, supervision, work policies, and working conditions. When these factors are affected negatively, you become dissatisfied with your work. Based on this analysis, a person can feel both satisfied and dissatisfied at work, but what keeps them going or forces them to leave is the balance and weighting factors that affect their decisions.

Process Theories

There are also four theories regarding the process of motivation, and they discuss **how** people get motivated.

1. Skinner's Reinforcement Theory

In his theory, Skinner proposes that the thing that motivates people to do something, or refrain from doing it, is its consequences. He explains that there are three ways you can create a behavior:

Positive reinforcement: This makes the person feel good about performing a certain behavior. For example, if you praise your child for waking up early or making their bed, you're using positive reinforcement to motivate them to repeat this behavior. It can be applied in the form of praise, gifts, money, promotion, or any other kind of appreciation.

Negative reinforcement: This motivates people to perform or not to perform a certain action, by giving them a reward that removes feelings of struggle. So when you give your hungry child some food only if they behave, you're motivating them to behave by removing the negative feeling; hunger.

Punishment: This prevents the undesired behavior with an undesired reinforcement. If a child makes a mess and is being noisy, and his mother shouts at him (negative verbal feedback) and punishes him by having him do the dishes (undesired reinforcement), then he becomes motivated to avoid making any more mess so he won't be punished again.

The ideal kind of reinforcement depends on the personality and character of the specific subject. But most psychologists prefer positive and negative reinforcements as opposed to punishment. While the first two reinforcements offer alternative behaviors, punishment doesn't offer any alternatives, breeds ill feelings and hatred toward the desired behavior, and doesn't really eliminate the behavior; it gets suppressed and pushed into the back of the person's mind.

2. Victor Vroom's Expectancy Theory

Vroom's theory suggests that whether or not we decide to take a certain action depends on what we expect to get out of it. We evaluate our actions before performing them (or, in other words, before feeling motivated to perform them) based on three factors:

Expectancy: The belief that by putting more effort into the task, we'll get better results. For example, if I put more effort into studying, I'll perform better on the test.

Instrumentality: The belief that the way we perform a certain action is directly related to the reward we'll get. So, if I perform better on the test, I'll get better results (the reward).

Valence: This factor affects how valuable the reward is for us. If I don't really think it's important whether or not I get better results on the test, I won't be motivated to perform the action anyway.

Vroom continues to explain that the extent of an individual's motivation can be calculated by multiplying the three factors together. If one or more factors are valued *zero*, then the individual won't be motivated at all.

3. Adam's Equity Theory

Adam tackles motivation from a different point of view. He proposes that people become motivated when they feel what they've put into a certain action is fairly compensated by its reward. If two employees put the same effort into a task, and the boss acknowledges the effort of one but not the other, the other will feel demotivated. When measuring the motivation of a person to perform his work, it was found that the person weighs the value of what they bring in—educational background, experience, skills, and talents—against what they receive—salary, promotions, rewards, development, etc. If what a person brings in overweighs the outcomes, they won't feel motivated.

4. Locke's Goal-Setting Theory

Locke offers another practical theory, which states that we'll become motivated when we set specific, realistic, and acceptable goals that we are committed to achieve. The stronger we want to achieve the goal, the bigger our motivation to see it through, and the stronger our commitment.

When we're focused on how we want our future to be, on our *goals* for the said future, we become motivated. These goals need to be specific, so just saying "I want to be happy" won't really motivate us. They also need to be realistic, as realistic goals will make us believe we can achieve them, while also imposing a certain level of difficulty that will challenge us in the process. Finally, we need to *accept* the goals we're setting.

If a certain goal is imposed on us, we won't be motivated to achieve it either.

Reflecting on the Motivation Theories

All of these theories are certainly mind-expanding, and they help us understand ourselves better. But what does all of this mean in real life?

The American Psychological Association has been trying to figure out how motivation really works in practical life. Most of these theories only focus on one aspect of life, like the content theories focusing primarily on our motivation in the workplace. Others discuss motivation irrelevant of age, gender, background, and individual differences. They've also found that motivation differs according to the field of study, so motivation in cognitive psychology is different from that in social or educational psychology. The experimentation methods also make a big difference in the results.

They've conducted several experiments, trying to assess how motivation affects the way we learn.

They've also researched how rewards, competition, and curiosity can affect our motivation level.

In brief, the conclusions they reached confirmed what we'd already believed: motivation helps you learn better. But they took it a step further and divided the source of our motivation to learn into two approaches: to master the subject, or to prove superior competency. When the motivation stems from our will to achieve mastery in a certain topic, the process of learning takes a longer time, but we become better at the subject. When it stems from our desire to compete and prove we're better than others, we take less time to achieve our goal, but it can easily be forgotten over time.

Moving on to how motivation is affected by certain factors, experiments have shown that reward, indeed, strengthens motivation. But the interesting part is when they've researched the effect of both extrinsic and intrinsic motivation on the individual. If you're motivated to work because of the salary, for example, then your motivation comes from the outside; it's extrinsic. When you're motivated to volunteer for a job because you *like* doing it, it's intrinsic motivation.

Research has shown how our motivation is directly affected by how much we like performing a certain action. If we don't like it at all, we're likely to run out of extrinsic motivation sooner or later. What's even more interesting is that, after extrinsic rewards are offered to those who'd previously been driven by intrinsic motivation, their motivation shifted to become extrinsic. They didn't *enjoy* performing the action as much as they used to, but rather, they started doing it for the reward.

This brings us to a scary conclusion. When we start doing what we like for an external reward instead of letting the action itself be our reward, our motivation shifts. Over time, we may stop performing the action altogether in the absence of any reward, and lose our valuable intrinsic motivation.

So perhaps, the key to sticking to our goals in the long run depends on our ability to nurture our intrinsic motivation. But research is still ongoing in this area, as there's a huge variety in how different human beings are motivated to think, act, and feel.

While we wait for the research to shed more light on this subject, there's another element to help us tackle our lack of motivation, which is known as willpower. So how exactly does this willpower work?

2. Willpower

People usually pursue motivation to be able to *enjoy* what they're doing, irrelevant of their motives. When they feel motivated to do something, chances are they'll perform better, feel the reward of their work paying off, and they'll *like* performing those tasks even more.

But we know from real-life experience that we can't depend on motivation. Sometimes—or most of the time—we have to do what we *need* to do, even if we don't feel like doing it. This is a virtue that most successful people would describe as having willpower. It is the secret technique they use to get things done, even when they least desire it.

Ever since the beginning of philosophy, the level of success and self-actualization has been evaluated by the strength of their willpower—starting from their early childhood. If you've been wondering what brought on such scientific assumptions, there's a very famous experiment known as the Marshmallow Test.

This experiment on our social behavior was conducted by Walter Mischel in the 1960s, who was then a professor at Stanford University. It went as follows: get a group of children, four to five years of age, and place a marshmallow on a plate in front of each one. Tell them you'll be leaving for 10 to 15 minutes, and that if you came back and found the marshmallow still intact, you'd give them another one. If we know one thing, that's how difficult it is going to be for a four-year-old to resist eating a marshmallow that's *right under their noses.*

As expected, most of the children weren't able to resist the temptation, but surprisingly, some were. The experiment was wrapped, only to be revisited by Mischel 40 years later. He became really curious about how those children grew up to be. Did the ability of some of the children to resist temptation and delay gratification do them any good in life? What he saw once he tracked down all of the subjects was that, yes, it made a significantly big difference.

He found that those who had patience, self-control, self-discipline, or *willpower*, had overall achieved greater success in life. They had better grades, got better jobs, had more stable relationships, better health, and were generally happier in their lives than those who gave in to temptation right away. So he concluded his experiment by assuming that willpower, or any of its synonyms, is the one true indication of what individuals will achieve in life—something that can be measured as early as four years of age.

But what is willpower? Are we just born with it—in which case it would be useless for those who don't have it to even try? Can we cultivate it? Is it the secret we've been telling you about, which you can use to turn your life around?

To put it simply, willpower is the ability to resist temptation when it arises, or to discipline yourself to perform an action even if you rather wouldn't. This power of self-control takes place in the prefrontal cortex of our brains, which is all about reasoning and decision-making. Science has studied how the human brain, specifically the prefrontal cortex, has evolved and grown around sixfold in size throughout the years. This is comforting, as it means that we have the ability to grow and nurture our willpower.

While willpower stems from the rational prefrontal cortex, there's an opposing force that we know as temptation. Temptation stems from the center of all emotions, impulses, desires, and instant gratifications: the amygdala. While we get really tempted to give in to our desires and instant gratification, our willpower tries to rationalize our actions.

*"There's a marshmallow that I can already feel melting in my mouth, I **need** to have it right away,"* the amygdala of a four-year-old would shout, but their prefrontal cortex would rationalize, *"I'll hold on for just a brief amount of time, and I'll get two marshmallows instead of one. It's worth the wait."*

This conflict between the two centers is described as hot (the instant gratification-driven amygdala) and cold (the rational, calm, and patient prefrontal cortex). The stronger our ability to rationalize over choosing instant rewards, the stronger our willpower, and the higher our chances of success in life.

Some might ask: *"So, if I have willpower, I can do absolutely anything in life, right? I can resist all temptations, and be successful and happy! Alright, where do I sign up?"*

As promising as that sounds, there's a catch. Willpower is not infinite. It's not something you acquire and maintain forever. In fact, the more willpower you spend, the faster it becomes depleted, and the easier you'll fall victim to temptation.

Picking up where Mischel left off, many studies have been conducted to further understand willpower. What a lot of studies concluded in common is that will power becomes depleted when you keep using it. In one experiment, individuals were asked to avoid thinking about white bears, as a form of thought-suppression. After the activity, they were offered beer to taste but were warned that they shouldn't drink too much, as they'll go through a driving test right after. The same warning was given to another group who hadn't undergone the thought-suppression activity. They found that the first group drank much more beer compared to the second group, confirming the effect of depleting willpower after a mentally (or, as other studies have shown, physically and emotionally) exhausting task. Even if the temptation would get them into trouble, they'd run out of most of their willpower to fight it off or rationalize.

There's an important rule when it comes to willpower, which is *use it or lose it.* If this rule sounds familiar, that's because it's the most common rule we hear when we hit the weights at the gym. Psychologists describe willpower as physicians would describe a muscle: the more you use it, the stronger it becomes. The more you neglect it, the weaker it gets. But even when we keep training it and increase our temptation-resisting threshold, it's bound to be depleted if we overuse it. According to the American Psychological Association, recent studies are yielding very interesting results. After studying many subjects who were depleted of willpower, they found that it seems as if their biological environment had changed. Some evidence points toward the possibility that the brain center related to cognition (the anterior cingulate cortex) starts to shut down, figuratively speaking. Other evidence suggests that the brain starts to run low on fuel, as exerting willpower forces the brain to use up its fuel, the blood sugar, much faster than normal.

On the other hand, they've discovered some evidence that suggests there are certain factors that delay willpower depletion, or even keep it in check. Such factors are the beliefs, attitudes, and internal workings of an individual. If a person is asked to keep their emotions in check while talking to a tiresome customer, their willpower becomes depleted. Meanwhile, if a person keeps their cool and tries to understand the customer, their willpower remains intact. They also suggest that our mood plays a big role in how strong our willpower is in a given situation.

Despite this evidence, research is also still ongoing. It's believed that willpower depletion can somehow be delayed by our personal beliefs, attitudes, and mood, but the fact remains that it's a finite resource that gets used up—it's only a matter of time. What this means is that we need to be smart in putting our willpower to use, and weigh up our options before we decide to spend it on certain actions.

3. Relapse

How many times have you heard stories of overweight people who decided to call on their willpower, find all the motivation in the world, shed pounds of excess fat, only to regain the weight after they've reached their goals—that is, if they haven't quit midway? How many times have you mustered every ounce of willpower you have to go to the gym? You went every day, pushed through the days you didn't feel like working out at all, started becoming motivated, and then one day, you just stopped. If motivation and willpower are the answers, why do we stop? Why don't we go forever?

While motivation and willpower are indeed two strong driving forces toward getting our lives together, achieving goals, and claiming success, studies have shown that we can't expect to solely depend on them for success. If they get removed from the equation—which is bound to happen at some point—we'll be left hopeless and stuck in place.

The fact remains that sometimes, we still fall apart, no matter how well we've been doing.

Sometimes a huge misfortune can occur, or we just wake up one day feeling completely demotivated. In those instances, what do we do? Does this mean we can't keep working or getting our lives together unless we feel motivated? If we deplete all of our willpower at work, does this mean that we should kiss losing weight or going to the gym goodbye?

We keep hearing stories every day about how successful, motivated, and strong-willed people suddenly fall off track. The fourth guy to walk into the bar, the one who turned his life around and became a rich, successful businessman, was able to make it out of his previous circumstances. And yet, he fell down. He relapsed.

That doesn't sound very promising.

A lot of credit has been given to willpower and how it can make or break our lives. But that was only the first half of the marshmallow story. Years after Mischel concluded his experiment, an NYU psychology professor, Tyler Watts, became very skeptical about those results.

For some reason, the Marshmallow Experiment had become very popular. Educational programs took its findings into account, and school curriculums were developed based on the assumptions. But a lot of criticism emerged against the theory, and it wasn't until Watts replicated the Marshmallow Experiment, experimenting with some control factors in the new run.

First of all, the original test was conducted on a very small number of children. Those children were all collected from Stanford's on-campus nursery school. Watts replicated the experiment to include children of various backgrounds, social groups, ethnicities, and household circumstances. The variation in the results was huge.

The new experiment shed light on the irrelevance of children's willpower to how well they perform later on in life. In fact, it tackled a deeper aspect of the study: those who were raised in poverty were much more likely to give in to temptation than those who were raised in financially stable households with higher educational levels. Which makes a lot of sense; how can you put candy in front of a candy-deprived child and expect them to delay their gratification? As far as their life experience goes, they won't get this chance ever again. They can't even trust the fact that they'll get a second marshmallow if they waited. Children who grew up in better economical settings weren't as deprived of marshmallow as their counterparts, so their ability to wait for a bigger reward was stronger. Even if they didn't get a second serving, they knew there were alternatives.

This replication brought the original findings into question. Most of us believe that willpower is, indeed, important; those who are able to focus on their priorities and aren't swayed by temptations are generally better at achieving their goals. But according to the recent findings, the relevance between how *naturally* strong-willed a child is and the probability of their future success is very uncertain. If anything, the study shows that future success depends largely on the background of the household the children grew up in.

What's even more uncertain is the direct relation between willpower and success. Before you get all confused, let's take a deeper look at the minds of self-proclaimed strong-willed people.

If we take the children in the previous experiment, for instance, we have those who resisted temptation and those who gave in. But don't you think that's somewhat unfair? To a child growing up in a rich household, candy was probably available any time. What if, at the time of the experiment, they just didn't feel like having any candy? What if they'd recently had one, or they simply didn't like marshmallows? Would it be fair to compare their behavior to another child who just *loved* marshmallows and hadn't had any for a while—and yet they resisted it anyway?

We've mentioned previously how willpower can be depleted easily. So, comparing two individuals who perform the same action, but ignoring the amount of struggle each of them had to go through to perform that action would just be unfair. What if going for a morning run just comes naturally to someone, but someone else needs a lot of pep talk and significant self-rewarding promises to go for the same morning run? The first person will be done with their task feeling refreshed, whereas the second one will feel all depleted.

This raises more uncertainty about willpower. The original studies focused more on those who exerted extreme self-control and restrain when faced with temptation. According to the initial findings, they were supposed to be more successful, happier, and focused in life. Guess what? They were not—not by any means.

Those who are more easily tempted, who put a lot of effort into keeping themselves in check, are usually the ones who fall back in no time. No matter how far they've managed to get, they fall away and maybe end up in a worse place than they'd started. A student on a scholarship can attend all lectures, work a part-time job to pay the rent and find the time to socialize and go to the gym. But when the time comes and they feel too pressured to keep holding everything in place, they'll let go of everything at once and relapse.

If willpower is under so much suspicion, then perhaps finding ways to motivate ourselves is the key? Unfortunately, this isn't the case either. While people often think of motivation as everlasting, our practical life proves it isn't. After all, motivation is only an emotion—it's not a skill you acquire.

While we know, based on experience, that we perform tasks perfectly when we feel motivated, and that depending on willpower is what gets us through our toughest days, we've now come to learn that they're both uncertain drivers toward success. There has to be something else; otherwise, how do some people manage to be sincerely happy with their lives?

Why can some achieve success and maintain a happy life, while others keep suffering as they struggle to reach their goals? Have I been wasting your time with all of these theories that don't really work in real life?

Before you start getting angry, I'll tell you what you've gained from this book so far. I'll also let you in on what scientific research in the last decade has managed to reveal. We've finally found out exactly what's missing—and how to make it work.

We've learned that motivation and willpower alone can't take us too far, and when they do, they eventually run out. But what we're about to learn is how using them to build healthy habits is a sure way to reach success, happiness, and everlasting peace.

So here's the answer we've all been looking for since the beginning: focusing on habits. In the following chapters, I'll take you through the journey of understanding habits, how they work, and the magic that building habits can bring into your life.

Part 3: Focus on Habits

Beyond Our Conscious Actions

One of the well-known stories in the medical literature is that of E.P., an amnesiac patient whose story starts in 1992. E.P. wasn't always amnesiac, he suffered from viral encephalitis one day at the age of 70. The virus ate away large parts of his medial temporal lobe, the part of the brain that's responsible for forming and storing long-term memories.

E.P. lost his memories all the way back into the 1920s. He couldn't recall anything that happened during these 50 years; he couldn't even recognize his grandchildren. He couldn't form any new memories either, as he'd keep forgetting everything that had just happened in a matter of seconds. Needless to say, he couldn't learn any new information.

One day, his wife moved him into a new neighborhood near their daughter. That way, they could be close to the team of medical researchers studying his case. She'd take him every day for a walk around the neighborhood, taking the same path every time. She'd show him around the house, every day, to get him snacks from the kitchen, or seat him in front of the TV to alleviate his boredom.

The scans of his brain had shown complete destruction of his medial temporal lobe, which made his chances of ever learning something new, or ever remembering any new memories, to be zero. But something happened that left the team of researchers astounded.

One day, E.P.'s wife couldn't find him in the house. She got frantic, called her daughter, and was just on her way to gather a search party for him when he walked back right into the house. He'd just went out for a walk. The same situation was repeated, but when they followed him, they found him following the same route his wife had taken him around. After closely monitoring his actions, they found out he was able to go to the kitchen on his own for a bowl of snacks. He'd find his way in front of the TV and open his favorite channel.

This didn't make any sense to the researchers. E.P. was, supposedly, unable to store any new information. They became even more confused when they asked him to describe the way to the kitchen, but he was left speechless. He didn't know how he got there; he just did.

The case of E.P. changed the way we understand how our brains work. It gave us valuable insight into the fact that there's another part of the brain that can store, use, and create new information, no matter how simple or complex this information may be. This part is the basal ganglia, and it's where all of our habits are stored.

If a completely amnesiac patient is able to form new routines and remember his way around in a totally unfamiliar neighborhood, then forming habits has nothing to do with our conscious decision-making process. As a matter of fact, 40% of our daily behavior is composed of habits; actions that we perform without any conscious thought, without any level of decision-making, and mostly, without even noticing we've taken action.

Let's think about it.

What do you think about when you're driving to work? You might tell me, *"the tasks I have for the day, an important meeting, and what I'll be having for lunch."* That's when I have to ask you again, what do you think about *when driving*? Do you make a conscious decision to take out your keys, start the engine, fix the mirrors, press on the clutch as you shift your gear to first (or reverse), and think of every step you need to take while driving? Do you even put any effort into finding your way to the office? Of course not. Not anymore, anyway.

When you first started learning how to drive, I'm sure you felt overwhelmed with every step you need to take. It took you some time, but now you're driving almost absent-mindedly. It's become natural for you to start the car and be on your way to work. It's become a *habit*.

Habits are so powerful because they work in the background. Even if you decide to take a new route today, you may very well find yourself, already midway to work, on the same old route you're used to taking. That's because our brain works in a very intriguing way.

Our brain is both magnificent and, well, pretty lazy. It's always looking for the shortest way to operate. It takes a lot of effort to develop new skills and memorize them, but it can't afford to be overwhelmed with the same input of information every day. That's why, instead of wasting a lot of energy on the same tasks, it stores them in the background. That way you can operate automatically on repetitive everyday tasks, and you can make room for new information and skills.

While there are habits that may seem pretty insignificant—like reaching out to the light switch without thinking, wearing socks and shoes in a specific order, and fixing your eyeglasses in the middle of a sentence—there are also habits that make a world of difference between where you are right now and where you want to go. How would you feel if, instead of feeling it's a daunting chore, you simply found yourself on your way to the gym every day after work? How would you feel if every single one of your goals became natural and *habitual* for you, in a way that you could go for everything you've ever wished to accomplish without giving it a second thought?

Forget giving yourself pep talks for hours on end in order to work out, or fighting so hard every day to stop yourself from smoking another cigarette. When our behavior becomes a habit, it takes away all of the conscious effort and willpower we'd otherwise need to perform the same action. Talk about saving energy!

So, what exactly are these magical things known as habits? Do we just need to repeat the same exercise over and over again till it becomes a habit? How many days will it take?

What Habits Are

Habits are behaviors we repeat on a regular basis without giving them any conscious thought. It's like being on autopilot, and this automaticity is what distinguishes habits. However, not everything we repeatedly do can be called a habit; habits are different from routines.

We have "routines" of what we're supposed to do. Our routines can be cleaning the house on the weekends, waking up at 6 a.m. in the morning to go to work, take a lunch break, drive back home from work. Most of the time, we go with the routine because we have to, not because we want to. Habits are the actions we carry out subconsciously. We can develop habits of checking the phone whenever a notification pops up, smoking a cigarette after eating, biting our nails when we're consumed in a task, or slouching our backs sitting in front of computers. Habits are behaviors, not a set-up routine. In this sense, our routines are filled with habits ranging all the way from tiny to significant.

When do we call certain habits *good*? When do we call them *bad*? What "annoying" habits do we have that we want to get rid of, and which combination of habits makes us who we are?

Habits are good for us when they affect us positively. If you develop a habit of keeping a straight back while working, going to the gym every day, eating healthy, or meditating, all of these habits reflect well on your health in one way or another. Habits are considered bad when they affect our overall health negatively; such as smoking excessively, putting our work off till the last minute, or eating junk food every day because it's practical.

Here's a list of some good habits you can develop for better health, success, and overall mental peace:

Working out regularly

Setting priorities

Getting a good night's sleep

Reading

Keeping a journal

Practicing mindfulness

Saving money

Having a hobby

Keeping a good posture

Eating healthy

On the other hand, here's a list of some bad habits that keep us stuck in an undesirable place:

Smoking

Procrastination

Wasting money impulsively

Eating junk food (or too much sugar, salt, etc.)

Stress eating

Nail biting

Being late

Overthinking

Staying in unhealthy environments or relationships

Exploding in anger

Whatever our collection of habits may be, they make us who we are at the moment. That doesn't mean they define us. The great thing about our brains is that we get to reprogram them. We have the amazing ability to replace our bad habits, build new ones that are beneficial to us, and even tweak the existing ones to our liking. But that's going to require some serious work, at least in the beginning. Once you're done, you'll go on autopilot, performing your habits like a pro.

For us to change, replace, or create habits, we first need to realize our existing ones. Next, we need to set goals for ourselves so we can know which habits to keep, discard, or build from scratch. That way, we can be on our way to creating the life of our dreams.

I have some really great news for you: we've already learned what it takes to figure out our existing habits. Remember our journey through self-awareness? Its purpose was to prepare you to be able to list your habits. You'll use what you've learned about being self-aware while listing your habits, analyzing and classifying them, and deciding whether or not you want to keep them.

In this part of our book, I'll take you on a tour to learn how our minds work: how we've built all of our habits, how we can change them and even build new ones. Once we understand how that works, we'll move on to goal-setting.

But first things first; how do habits work?

The Habit Loop

Through studying E.P.'s behavior vigorously, researchers were able to define, precisely, how habits are formed.

They found that habits are formed by repeating the same behavior regularly, but that's not the only secret to forming habits. Going to the gym every day won't make it a habit. However, going to the gym every day after getting back from work *can* make it a habit. Going to the gym every day after getting back from work, and feeling good as a result of your workout, every day, *is going to* make it a habit.

It may seem like there's no difference in these three scenarios, but those slight variations make all the difference to our brains.

For our brain to record a habit, it needs an **environmental cue**. If we take the previous example, it's *getting back from work*. Whenever that cue is present, our brain goes on autopilot to perform the **behavior** that is recorded as a habit. But that isn't enough for our brain to turn that behavior into a habit; it needs motivation, it needs to get a **reward** out of this behavior. The reward, in this case, is feeling good after the workout session. And this reward becomes the **craving** the brain feels every time it's introduced to the environmental cue.

When we repeat the same behavior enough for our brain to memorize the link between the *cue* we'd set up and the *behavior* we want it to remember, and link the *reward* with the behavior every time we're developing a habit, the brain will work on autopilot. Every time you get back from work, your brain will be looking forward to getting the reward, so you'll find yourself on your way to the gym in no time— *without putting any effort into making the decision to go.*

That's the same strategy we use while training our pets to exhibit certain behaviors. If I'm training my cat to come sit on my lap whenever I whistle, I'm making the whistle its cue. But if you know anything about cats, you'll know that they don't like being told what to do (pretty much like most of us). So, I offer it a treat, but I don't give the treat unless it does what I want it to do: come sit on my lap. By repeating the same cue over and over again and offering the same reward every time, the behavior becomes natural. In its mind, the whistle means treats. That's exactly how our minds work.

When we're introduced to the same cue over and over again, and we perform a certain action that's followed by a reward, it becomes automatic. Every time there's a cue, our brain starts craving its reward. It only has to execute a certain action to get this reward, and so it does.

Environmental Cues

Environmental cues can be found everywhere around us. When you enter your room, you reach out for the light switch right away. When you arrive at work, you prepare your coffee. When it's lunchtime, you buy a can of soda to drink with your meal. When the meeting ends and your boss assigns you the tasks, you get to work. When you wake up every day, you go to the bathroom, wash your face and brush your teeth.

However, your brain doesn't get into habit-mode every time a cue presents itself. If you wake up after a nap in the middle of the day, do you go brush your teeth? If you walk around the kitchen first thing in the morning instead of going directly to the bathroom, do you still brush your teeth in the kitchen? If it's 2 p.m. and your room is filled with daylight, do you still reach for the light switch as soon as you enter it?

An environmental cue isn't just about the place you've associated with the action. It takes into account all of the environmental cues: actions, time, place, external and internal cues, and even the chain of habits associated with this specific behavior.

To explain it in more detail, you only brush your teeth:

After you wake up (action)

In the morning (time)

In the bathroom (place)

To feel your teeth are cleaner, to get rid of morning breath (internal cues)

After you wash your face (chain of habits)

As we go about our days, every single second of it, our brains are always looking for cues. Well, they're looking for rewards to be more specific, but the brain keeps searching for cues so it can get its reward. Every time it associates a cue with its consecutive reward as a result of repetitive behavior, it gets stored eventually. Whenever the cue presents itself at the right time, in the right place, and under the right circumstances, the habit is built.

Cravings

Our brain keeps looking for cues to get its reward. Even if there's no cue, it keeps on searching. We can describe this activity in other words: the brain *craves* the reward. And once the cue got associated with its reward, the brain has been craving it ever since.

Without craving that feeling, thought, experience, or reward, the brain won't keep looking for cues. It will feel that going on autopilot to perform a behavior is not worth the bother. We don't create habits for the behavior itself, but we rather create them for the rewards we're going to get out of them. And that's what craving is all about.

Every time you smoke a cigarette, you're not smoking because you like to ingest some carbon monoxide into your lungs. You smoke because it helps you feel more relaxed, alert, and focused. That's why, despite the label on the pack warning you of cancer, you still go for a cigarette. The instant reward outweighs the long-term risks you're taking, and that's exactly what your brain is craving: instant rewards. Drug addiction works the same way. Someone who's built a nail-biting habit every time they're engrossed in a task, watching TV, or in a frustrating situation will crave the stress relief they get through biting their nails. We brush our teeth every day when we wake up to feel refreshed, and after every meal or before we go to bed because we crave the feeling of cleanliness.

Cravings work in different ways for everyone. Just because someone keeps craving the high of working out doesn't mean that the next person would have the same cravings. Some people constantly crave chocolate while others can't even get themselves to eat it (I have no idea how, to be honest). The smell of doughnuts can trigger the craving inside one person's brain, but for another, it's a painful reminder of a bad breakup beside a doughnut shop. The smell of doughnuts is an environmental cue for both people in this case, tempting the first to satisfy their craving by indulging in a doughnut, and motivating the other to stay away from the doughnut shop to avoid reliving painful memories.

Environmental cues awaken the emotional experience that a person has associated with them. This emotional experience is what we call craving. When our emotional experience of carrying out a certain action is positive, it becomes something our brains keep looking forward to repeating. In that case, we keep craving to eat the doughnut, smoke the next cigarette, get a dose of drugs, drink alcohol, bite our nails, brush our teeth or go to the gym. When our emotional experience associated with the behavior is negative, we build habits to stop or avoid those feelings. We avoid the doughnut shop, the burden of exercise, the stress of confrontation, and we even get back to using drugs to avoid the pain of withdrawal.

Our cravings are either emotional or physical in nature—and sometimes it's both. When it comes to using drugs, there's usually an additional factor of physical dependency, which makes it even harder to break this addictive habit. When a person uses drugs for the first time, they experience a very pleasurable feeling. This emotional and physical experience creates cravings; the emotional craving is the pleasurable feeling itself, and the physical craving is the effect of chemicals in the bloodstream.

Overcoming drug addiction is remarkably more difficult than breaking most habits due to the physical dependency it creates. The body stops releasing its feel-good chemicals; specifically a neurotransmitter called dopamine, which is responsible for our good mood. This makes the craving for drugs much stronger, as its reward is much stronger as well. If an addict tries to quit suddenly, they experience very painful withdrawal symptoms. That's why the chances of relapse are very strong with physical dependence; the body is craving an end to this painful experience—even if it's for the better in the long run. It doesn't care, it just wants the pain to stop, so the addict relapses into using drugs once again.

Behavior

If you're free to choose any behavior in the world to make it a habit, what would you choose? Before you start daydreaming, let's take a step back. How do you decide on which habits to make, which to keep and which to bid farewell to? Picking a random behavior and saying you want to make it a habit won't really work. Well, you *can* make it a habit by following the steps, but what good will it generally do you in your life?

The whole point of focusing on habits is because it's the ultimate technique we can use to change our lives for the better. But if we have no idea what "better" means, specifically, we won't be going a long way. Instead of choosing a certain behavior and working on it, it's much more effective to set up our goals for where we want to go. Once we have a clear vision of the end of the tunnel, choosing our habits will work best in our favor.

However, choosing a goal isn't enough on its own. If our goals don't intersect together to create the lifestyle we desire, it will feel like we're barking up the wrong trees all at once. Our efforts will be scattered, we'll be unfocused, and we'll have no idea what the greater picture we're building is. Don't get me wrong, there will be some periods in our lives that we have no idea what we want from this world. Being lost is nothing to be ashamed of. But if, during that confusing period, we set our goal to be *"figuring out what I want to be and do,"* then it's the best anyone can ask for. You'll focus all of your efforts on getting those answers, so when you do, you'll be able to set clear goals that you know for sure are going to work for you.

This collection of goals that aim for the integrative design of our desired future life can be called a system. The system encompasses all of our goals, explains how they connect together, how they're broken down into smaller goals that are further broken down until we can identify small tasks we can complete daily. These tasks are the behavior we'll focus on turning into habits. And this system is what we'll call our lifestyle.

Rewards

Rewards, however, can be tricky. Let's take the gym example. Instead of considering *feeling good about working out* as the reward, let's say we decided to give ourselves a treat, like *I'll buy myself new clothes*. But what exactly is stopping me from buying new clothes if I *don't* work out? Another catch is that, am I supposed to buy myself new clothes for every single day I work out?

Some would argue that, no, I'll reward myself with new clothes once I reach a certain goal from working out; a certain fitness level or losing X pounds of weight. While that *might* work as a motivating goal, it's no good for building a habit out of working out.

For rewards to really work in building habits, they need to comply with three rules:

They have to be related to the behavior.

They need to come directly after the behavior.

They should be small rewards.

The first rule is that they have to be related to the behavior. This makes sense to our brains, and think about it: if I decide to buy new clothes, then there's nothing stopping my brain from skipping workouts and going straight to the mall to get me the new clothes. The reward has to be something that you *have* to perform the behavior in order to receive. You won't feel good if you don't work out. There's a juice bar right next to the gym, so you can't treat yourself to your favorite juice unless you go to the gym. There's a hot new guy at the gym, so you won't be able to show off unless *you actually go to the gym.*

The second rule of rewards is that they need to be presented directly after the behavior. If your brain doesn't get that instant reward after executing the action, it won't stick. If it doesn't get the reward *every time* after the action, it won't form the habit. The whole idea of forming habits, for our brain, is that it gets something out of the behavior. It recognizes the cue, and cue equals reward. If it doesn't build this path between cue and reward, there's no way it's going to keep performing that behavior for nothing. Remember cats. Brains are just spoiled little cats.

The third rule states that rewards should be small—wait, what? If our brains are just like cats, wouldn't it make more sense that a bigger reward would motivate them to form a habit better, or faster—however brains do their thing? It figures that a reward shouldn't *motivate* the behavior, it's only there to *reinforce* it.

To explain how smaller rewards work better in creating habits, we'll need to revisit something we've mentioned while talking about motivation. Remember how we explained that there are two types of motivation: intrinsic and extrinsic? Intrinsic motivation helps us carry out actions because we get internal rewards out of them. We feel good when we're doing it, we *enjoy* doing it. Extrinsic motivation is the reward we get from our outer environment, which also helps us execute the action. The main difference between these two kinds of motivation is that we're bound to keep performing the action driven by intrinsic motivation, but if the reward is taken out of extrinsic motivation, there's a much higher chance we'll stop executing the action.

The same goes for building habits. If the reward is too big compared to the behavior, we'll start exhibiting the behavior just to get the reward.

And what happens if one day I don't have enough money to get myself new clothes after hitting the gym? I won't get the reward my brain has associated with exercise. Brain error 404.

There's actually a very thin line between performing a behavior for the reward and doing it for the sake of enjoying the behavior. When you build habits on behaviors you already enjoy, the possibility of sticking to this habit becomes much higher. On the other hand, if you decide on a behavior that you absolutely despise, there's not a very good probability you'll keep it.

Did this sound worrying? This might mean that there's *no way on earth* for us to make a habit of what we need to do to be successful. Most of us don't enjoy working, working out, eating healthy, or limiting distractions. This is where I tell you that it's all about what we *think* about the behavior. If I go to the gym thinking about how much I hate working out every step of the way, there's no way I'll be getting any rewards out of it. If I go to work every day hating the environment, my coworkers, my boss, and even the work itself, there's no way I'll get to set up habits of completing my tasks.

The way we think of any activity can make or break the habit. Instead of thinking about how much I'm suffering throughout the workout, if I can find some good aspects—like my heart feels better, I can climb the stairs without gasping for breath like a dying person—and if the workout itself is actually fun, then my brain shifts the way it sees that workout entirely. It starts looking forward to it. If there's something I can do about my work environment to make me feel better, the same will happen. If it's completely hopeless, perhaps it's time for a change.

It's beautiful and pretty amazing how the human brain can be rewired. We can change where we are. We have the ability to shift the way we think about different things. Even the most persistent of habits, those actions that we carry out without even realizing, can be changed when we know the tricks. Where we are isn't destined, we aren't defined by our genetics and the way we've been raised. Yes, all of those factors play a big role in creating versions of our current selves, but even that can be changed. *We* are able to change that.

So, the next time you want to start doing something you need to do and make a habit of it, think of your cues and rewards. Instead of mustering all of your willpower to repeat the action, even on your worst days, channel that willpower into building the link between cues and behaviors.

Belief

The habit loop consists of four steps: a cue, a craving, a behavior, and a reward. But there's one more important factor without which our chances of relapse become so much higher. The last and most important factor in building habits that stick, is to *believe* you can stick to your habits. It's the factor of belief.

Belief doesn't indicate a certain religion or spiritual rituals. It refers to your ability to believe in the habits you're building. Let me ask you, why do you want to build new habits? Why do you want to get rid of the old ones?

Most of us would reply to those questions with similar answers. *We want to improve our lives. We want to stop hurting ourselves with our bad habits. We want to be in control.* But why is it that so many of those who have managed to turn their lives around through new habits still relapse? Why do they go back to their old habits even if there's no physical dependency, or if they've already overcome it?

This can be explained by how rehab centers treat their patients. Or more specifically, how Alcoholics Anonymous (AA) was able to help alcoholics overcome their addiction and achieve lesser rates of relapse than any other rehab program before them. AA has 12 steps to sobriety, and if you go through them, they're all revolved around believing in God and giving Him the higher power over us. Scientists and researchers were very skeptical. You can't really go and tell a scientist that God is the answer, but real-life results showed differently. So where was the magic coming from?

After AA established that their program really does work miracles, scientists were very curious to learn the secret. So they dug deeper into the psychological effects of the program and they were able to find the answer. AA's rules are all built on the importance of belief. Most of those seeking alcohol, drugs, or any other means of addiction had usually chosen that path to escape from what they were going through. Some sought alcohol for pain relief, some sought drugs for feelings of euphoria, but what they had in common was the craving for a pleasurable feeling when life went very wrong.

We keep hearing about many people who'd achieved years of sobriety, but somehow they fell into a deep pit of addiction once again. That usually occurs when something tragic happens in their lives. Our brains never forget any habits. All of the old ways are still wired, we've just managed to overwrite them with new paths. But the old ones still exist, and sometimes, all it takes is the wrong motivation to backslide.

And so they relapse. Deep inside, they don't believe there's a way out. They don't believe they can make it through without the help of those substances. They think they *need* to drink, use drugs, escape into sex, gambling, or any other destructive habit they'd given up after years of reprogramming their brains. They lack the most important factor to keep their habits around; the belief that they can make it through without addiction.

That's why AA's principles are so effective. They give people an alternative hope when all goes wrong. The people believe they can make it through, that they have what it takes to get through the rough patch. And they do. Today, there are many different organizations that have tweaked AA's principles to some extent to fit different segments of people. Some organizations offer rehab programs for drug addicts, others for sex, gambling, and every other addiction out there. They're not all focused on Christianity. But they all have one thing in common: they give people a belief system they can lean on during their hardest days.

The Habit Loop Worksheet

Habit #1:

The cue:

The craving:

The behavior:

The reward:

Habit #2:

The cue:

The craving:

The behavior:

The reward:

Habit #3:

The cue:

The craving:

The behavior:

The reward:

Habit #4:

The cue:

The craving:

The behavior:

The reward:

Habit #5:

The cue:

The craving:

The behavior:

The reward:

Tampering with Our Habits

We've come to understand how habits work, but how do we turn this knowledge into practical, easy-to-follow, clear steps?

We know that the four steps of forming habits are:

The cue

The craving

The behavior

The reward

It stands to reason that we're going to tackle these four steps when creating or changing habits.

If we want to build new habits, we first need to pave the way, before jumping into the habit. To do that, we'll first need to choose a cue that's quite obvious and easy to notice. We'll analyze our days and routines, and recognize different cues we can use to our advantage. Next is building the feelings of craving, which need to be attractive. The behavior comes next, and it needs to be small, easy, and realistic. If you choose unrealistically big behaviors, the effort they require will outweigh both the cravings and the rewards. Your chances of sticking to them will be slim, and even slimmer will be the chances of them ever becoming habits. Finally, you need to make the reward satisfying, but not overly satisfying. You don't want to start performing the behavior for the reward, and risk never making a habit of it. We can sum this up in four words:

Make it *obvious, attractive, simple, and satisfying.*

And if that's what it takes to form a habit, then we just need to do the opposite to break habits. Instead of an obvious cue presenting itself, we'll make it fade into the background. The easiest way to do that is to change our routine or tweak it enough so we can't recognize the cue anymore. We'll make the craving become unattractive. If you have a habit of smoking, focus more on how it makes your breath smell bad. If you're addicted to sugar, remind yourself of the weight you're gaining. Next comes the behavior, which you'll make much more difficult to perform. So, in order to smoke a cigarette, you'll need to go the extra mile to get it from a specific store, or work in a non-smoking environment. As for the reward, you'll make it unsatisfying. Instead of going for your favorite chocolate, plan your habit to visit the store that doesn't sell your favorite brand. In four adjectives, we can sum it up as follows:

Make it *invisible, unattractive, difficult, and unsatisfying*.

Building New Habits

Building new habits are much more difficult than changing existing ones. That's because it's much easier to reprogram the brain into changing a behavior once it's already established the connection between cues, cravings, and rewards. It's not impossible to create a new habit loop, it's just going to need more time and conscious effort.

The smartest thing to do is to hack existing habits. If you have a bad habit, exchange it with a better behavior using the same cues and rewards, in a way that you'll keep craving the effect of the habit. Instead of smoking a cigarette first thing at work, go for a cup of coffee. The caffeine will give you a mental boost that is similar to the one you get from nicotine; you'll get your reward while keeping the craving. If you already have an established routine of habits, then slip in an extra one. If you have a morning routine of waking up, stretching in bed, washing your face and brushing your teeth, try to slip in a session of meditation or yoga. As soon as you wake up, transition from your stretching into breathing exercises, full-body stretching, and then go on with the rest of the routine. If you want to remember to take your vitamins in the morning, put them beside your water bottle, keys, and sunglasses. That way you'll remember them every time you're about to leave, because your already-established routine will remind you.

Let's get into more practical examples of good habits and how to establish them. I've created a list of habits that I consider good, but good habits are countless. All I'm trying to do is give you a breakdown of real-life examples, and then it will be up to you to create your own habits and stick to them. For every habit, I'm going to answer five questions:

Why is this a good habit?

What's the cue?

What's the reward?

What craving does this behavior satisfy?

How to start the behavior?

Let's get started!

Why is this a good habit?

Working out has been proven, over and over again, to improve your health. It helps maintain good blood pressure levels, strengthens your muscles, and works your heart and lungs properly. That way, oxygen is delivered easily to every cell of your body. Working out helps us keep our bodies in their best shape and that doesn't merely mean losing weight or building muscles.

An added benefit of exercise is how our bodies react to it. By working out regularly, the body starts secreting endorphins. These are natural opioids delivered to our bodies by our bodies. Talk about a natural high! All of these benefits reflect greatly on our lives; they help us focus on work, endure more stress, and have more energy to fully enjoy our lives.

What's the cue?

After going through your daily routine, try to fit in a fixed time for working out. Let's say as soon as you get back from work, or first thing in the morning before going to work. Whichever works for you. The only rule is to make the cue obvious and to repeat the same circumstances you're choosing every day.

What's the reward?

Working out comes with a lot of intrinsic rewards, so that's a great bonus. You can choose your own reward: the natural high, the increased threshold of enduring stress, enhanced focus, or feeling healthier and more alive. (Hint: you can check all of the boxes!)

What craving does this behavior satisfy?

In this case, you have a craving for feeling good after working out (due to the sense of achievement and the endorphins), and you're craving the control you have over your body and mind.

How to start the behavior?

Remember, small but sure steps. You can choose the workout settings that work best for you. Many prefer to work out in the comfort of their homes, and there are many home workout programs out there to get you started. Others get more motivated by going to the gym, getting a personal trainer, or tagging along with their friends. Once again, choose whatever works best for you. Don't try to jump straight into complex workout routines, which is a principle you'll learn anyway if you choose a home workout program or train with a personal trainer. You can start with a 10-minute morning workout every day, go for a walk, or do some beginner-level yoga. You'll find yourself ready to upgrade the intensity the second week, and then upgrade some more in the third week. Before you know it, you'll be on your way!

Setting Priorities

Why is this a good habit?

When we don't have clearly set priorities, we go wherever the wind takes us. Our efforts are scattered, and as a result, we can't achieve any goals. Making a habit of setting our priorities is one of the best steps to getting our lives back together. It also helps us overcome procrastination.

What's the cue?

Some like to start with a morning meditation, ending it with a session of listing their priorities for the day. Others like to end every day by checking off the finished tasks and creating the next day's to-do list. Some do that as soon as they get to work. How would listing priorities fit in your own routine?

What's the reward?

There's a sense of achievement you get every time you list what you have to do; it makes you feel organized. It also helps you arrange your day and schedule, so you know from the beginning how to manage your time. The end reward is getting closer to your goals, which you can measure by recording the steps you've taken that day in the direction of your set goal.

What craving does this behavior satisfy?

The craving you'll be feeling is for having everything under control; having a plan you can follow to ensure success.

How to start the behavior?

I like to keep a small notebook with me at all times to list my tasks for the day; I'm a bit old school when it comes to these things. But there are countless mobile applications to help you with productivity and listing tasks.

Why is this a good habit?

Getting enough sleep is essential for our body systems to work efficiently. Sleeping for at least seven to eight hours every day has also been shown to reduce stress levels, increase focus, and boost our immune system.

What's the cue?

If you have problems sleeping well, we'll need to revisit your routine. Why are you struggling to sleep? Are you overwhelmed with work? Trust me, your work will be affected much worse if you keep compromising your sleep. Do you have a habit of losing track of time while watching shows or checking social media? If so, then it's a habit you need to break.

To get enough hours of sleep, you should sync your sleeping schedule with your work. Let's say you need to wake up at 7 a.m. every morning. But somehow, you lose track of time and sleep at 2 or 3 a.m. To create a new habit of sleeping well, your cue would be at 11 p.m. It can come after a meditation session, listing your tasks, reading for a while, or even watching some episodes of your favorite show. Be warned that if the activity you're engaging in right before bed is too interesting, sleeping right away won't sound like a very attractive idea, and you'll likely lose track of time. If you can't keep temptations under control yet, it would be smarter to leave the interesting activities to the weekends.

What's the reward?

You'll experience enhanced mental focus, physical strength, and immunity to diseases.

What craving does this behavior satisfy?

I can't believe I have to explain why getting enough sleep is important, I mean... it's sleep! It's heaven on earth. You'll keep craving this feeling of rest and peace.

How to start the behavior?

The first step to starting the behavior is to set your cues right, and keep temptations in check. Some people have much more difficulty falling asleep as a result of anxiety, depression, or other factors. In this case, they must deal with those factors first.

Reading

Why is this a good habit?

Reading enriches your mind, soul, and creativity. It opens a whole world of possibilities you never knew existed, but those who came before you have stumbled upon and described in their own words. It keeps you well aware of your surroundings, yourself, and others.

What's the cue?

Is it on your lunch break? When you get back home after work? Is it what you do while drinking your morning coffee? Any set period of time when you'd be able to immerse yourself in a good book can be the perfect cue.

What's the reward?

The reward you'll get, aside from feeling sophisticated, is a sense of achievement. Depending on what you're reading, your mind can go to very different places.

What craving does this behavior satisfy?

This habit mainly satisfies your curiosity, and that's probably a feeling you'll keep craving.

How to start the behavior?

tart your reading habits by preparing a comfortable environment. Get your cup of drink ready, set the lighting and temperature to your liking, and settle comfortably into a sofa or a chair. You'll definitely be reading about the topics you're most interested in, so choose something that sparks your curiosity and sense of creativity.

Why is this a good habit?

No matter how small your current salary is, there's probably some amount of money you'd be able to save. Saving money will help you face your future better, providing you with more means to live comfortably and get what you desire. Whether you're dreaming of a car, your own apartment, new clothes, or a vacation, saving money will help you every step of the way.

What's the cue?

Your cue would be to log the price every time you buy something or spend any money.

What's the reward?

The reward will be the feeling of achievement you get when you stick to a plan. Counting the money you'll be saving is also a great incentive!

What craving does this behavior satisfy?

You've been craving for that feeling of financial comfort for way too long. Once you actually start saving money, it becomes addictive!

How to start the behavior?

This can be a bit tricky, as we'll tackle both the impulses that tempt you to waste money, and where they fit in your routine. But first there's something we need to know: where does all your money go? Do you spend it on transportation? Is it wasted on junk food and takeout? Cigarettes? Drinks? Outings? You might have a general idea, but that's not enough. The best thing to do is to set up a routine of logging all of your expenses during the month. There are some really good mobile applications for that, or you can go old school and document it in your journal.

To start, you'll set down your salary first, and then you'll list all of your essential needs for the week. If you can categorize them that would also help a lot. It can go something like this:

Household items

Personal hygiene

Entertainment

Transportation and gas

Other essentials

Then you calculate the needs in each category, and every time you buy something, you log it. This way, you'll know how much allowance you have left in each category. Some people specify a certain amount of money to go into savings based on their expenses, and I recommend you do the same.

If you find your expenses to be way too high, then you'll need to start optimizing the way you spend money. If you find out that you're wasting money on fast food, perhaps you should prepare homemade food in lunch boxes on your weekend to take with you to work. If a lot of money goes to household items, compare your options and go for items that cost less without compromising quality or efficiency. If a specific item is essential to you, then try to find a more cost-effective alternative or brand. If it's not essential, then you'll need to start gradually cutting it off.

At the end of the day, starting or ending any habit needs a lot of willpower and conscious effort to rewire your brain. Planning out a routine on paper will help.

Building New Habits Worksheet

Habit #1:

Why is this a good habit?

What's the cue?

What's the reward?

What craving does this behavior satisfy?

How to start the behavior?

Habit #2:

Why is this a good habit?

What's the cue?

What's the reward?

What craving does this behavior satisfy?

How to start the behavior?

Habit #3:

Why is this a good habit?

What's the cue?

What's the reward?

What craving does this behavior satisfy?

How to start the behavior?

Habit #4:

Why is this a good habit?

What's the cue?

What's the reward?

What craving does this behavior satisfy?

How to start the behavior?

Habit #5:

Why is this a good habit?

What's the cue?

What's the reward?

What craving does this behavior satisfy?

How to start the behavior?

Getting Rid of Bad Habits

Habits can't be forgotten; they can only be ignored, changed, or replaced. While building new habits is much more difficult than changing or replacing a pre-existing habit, getting rid of our bad habits can be pretty tricky too. The longer we've maintained the habit, the harder it is to break. It's even harder when the cravings are strong. Unfortunately, I won't be able to guide anyone in overcoming habits that stem from physical dependence. They'll need help from certified professionals, who will also be able to guide them through overcoming bad habits at the later stages.

As for all the other habits we keep struggling with, there are two ways to hack into them. We either break the routine or replace the habit. To do that, we'll ask ourselves one question, and depending on the answer, we'll proceed with five others:

Can I replace this habit with a good one?

If your answer is yes, then you'll use the same habit loop, but tamper with the behavior you want to change. If the answer is no, then you'll work on breaking the chain of steps in the loop as we've mentioned before. You'll hide the cue, make the craving unattractive, make the behavior more difficult to perform and let the reward be unsatisfying.

Your next set of questions will be as follows:

How is this habit affecting me negatively?

What's the cue?

What's the reward?

What craving does this behavior satisfy?

How do I break the habit?

Once we answer these questions, we'll have much more clarity and strength to face our bad habits and break them for good.

Smoking

How is this habit affecting me negatively?

Smoking affects your health dramatically. It weakens your heart and destroys your lungs over the years, and might cause you to feel exhausted on a daily basis. Not to mention it's a black hole of wasting money.

What's the cue?

Your cue can be waking up, drinking your morning coffee, going to work, ending your meal, or ending your day. It can even be the smell of smoke or the sight of someone lighting up a cigarette.

What's the reward?

Smoking gives you a boost of nicotine, which supposedly kick-starts your mind and soothes your mood.

What craving does this behavior satisfy?

Every time you are exposed to the cue, your brain starts craving the rewards you get from smoking.

How do I break the habit?

The best course of action when it comes to overcoming nicotine addiction is to break away from your current cues. You'll also need to tamper with the steps of the habit loop.

If you frequent smoking areas, try to change your hangouts and company. If your main cue is a situation at work and you're craving the mental boost, make yourself a cup of coffee, eat an apple, or go for a walk on your break. Instead of taking the route where you pass by the store to get your cigarettes on your way to work, change your route. Find other ways to satisfy the craving and rewards you get from smoking, and make it more difficult to get your hands on any cigarettes.

Bad Eating Habits

How is this habit affecting me negatively?

Bad eating habits include many behaviors such as eating junk food, eating too much of a certain type of food, binge eating, or stress eating. All of these habits affect your health negatively in both the short and long run. Eating unhealthy food that's filled with way too much oil, fat and sodium can be detrimental to your blood pressure and arteries. It gradually clogs the arteries, which may result in serious heart conditions. On the other hand, most unhealthy and processed foods play a main factor in gaining weight. The same goes for binge eating and stress eating.

What's the cue?

If your cue is related to boredom, stress, or being too engulfed in work, then your cue may simply be your routine: setting up your studying space, arriving at work and getting started on tasks, being home on the weekend and watching TV, having too much free time on your hands, etc.

In the case of junk food and processed sugar, then once again, it's all in your routine. Do you order junk food because you didn't prepare any homemade food? Are you used to ending your meal with a bar of chocolate? Do you always drink your tea/coffee with a lot of sugar? There you go, you have your cues.

What's the reward?

The first reward we get from eating is feeling happy, which is mainly the work of a chemical called serotonin. Serotonin plays an important role in regulating our mood and mental functions, but it also makes us feel happy whenever we eat something that tastes good. Our taste buds would agree!

What craving does this behavior satisfy?

We crave food to satisfy our hunger with something tasty, which can be the case of junk food—because let's admit it, that thing is delicious! But stress-eating habits usually have little to do with satisfying hunger. They serve to alleviate the mood we're stuck in, whether it's stress, boredom, or anxiety. And that's the craving we feel every time we get into that mood: getting rid of these uncomfortable emotions.

How do I break the habit?

It all depends on which rewards and cravings trigger your bad eating habits, but you can definitely get over them. You'll need to work both on breaking your routine and replacing bad habits in this case.

Instead of putting processed sugar in your tea or coffee, perhaps you can consider putting honey or another natural alternative; they're healthier but give a similar taste. Some decide to quit sugar altogether, and some give up on tea and coffee for the sake of this. Instead of eating junk food for lunch every day, perhaps you can prepare yourself homemade meals in your free time. If you're used to eating a bar of chocolate after your meals, why not substitute it with natural, healthy, and tasty fruits?

If your bad eating habits are stemming from stress eating, then a break in the routine might be the answer. When you're bored, how about you go for another activity that takes your mind off food? You can go out with friends, pick up a book, or engage in your hobbies. If you're used to eating while working or studying because it helps you focus, then why not change what you're eating? Instead of nibbling on fries, prepare a bowl of veggies, some air-popped popcorn, or any other healthy, low-calorie food.

Nail Biting

How is this habit affecting me negatively?

The mildest effect of nail biting is a bad appearance. However, when the habit gets out of control, it can result in pain, damage and infection around the nails. Plus, exposing yourself directly to all the bacteria on your hands might not be the best idea.

What's the cue?

Do you start biting your nails when you become engrossed in a task? Does it mostly happen when you're watching TV? Your cue may be taking notice of a broken or chipped nail, and sometimes a frustrating social situation.

What's the reward?

Your reward can be a feeling of achievement after you've evened out your nails, which can indicate a mild level of OCD. In the case of a stress-related habit, it serves as a method for soothing your nerves when faced with a daunting task or an uncomfortable situation.

What craving does this behavior satisfy?

You're probably craving the absence of an uncomfortable feeling, such as stress, anxiety or boredom. You may also be craving the sense of achievement you get when you've completed biting all parts of your nails.

How do I break the habit?

If you starting biting your nails to even out the chipped and broken parts (but keep going until the free edge is all gone), then perhaps you can carry a nail clipper or trimmer with you at all times. Natural oil treatments are also great for strengthening nails against breaking. If it's the result of dealing with stress, anxiety, or boredom, then you'll need to find another way to get a similar sense of relaxation in exchange for biting your nails. You can try keeping a journal by your side, and every time you feel tempted to bite your nails, you can record your feelings instead.

Sometimes two people exhibit the same behavior, but they're driven by different cravings and seeking different rewards. There's no need to mention that the cues are also different for everyone. If one or more of the examples I've given doesn't work for you, that's completely normal. After all, you know yourself best. But you can always find guidance in these examples regarding the pattern of thoughts to go through and the steps to take in order to figure out what works for you. In the end, that is the whole point of this exercise.

Replacing Old Habits Worksheet

Habit #1:

Can I replace this habit with a good one?

How is this habit affecting me negatively?

What's the cue?

What's the reward?

What craving does this behavior satisfy?

How do I break the habit?

Habit #2:

Can I replace this habit with a good one?

How is this habit affecting me negatively?

What's the cue?

What's the reward?

What craving does this behavior satisfy?

How do I break the habit?

Habit #3:

Can I replace this habit with a good one?

How is this habit affecting me negatively?

What's the cue?

What's the reward?

What craving does this behavior satisfy?

How do I break the habit?

Habit #4:

Can I replace this habit with a good one?

How is this habit affecting me negatively?

What's the cue?

What's the reward?

What craving does this behavior satisfy?

How do I break the habit?

Habit #5:

Can I replace this habit with a good one?

How is this habit affecting me negatively?

What's the cue?

What's the reward?

What craving does this behavior satisfy?

How do I break the habit?

Goal Setting

Our final stop in this book is setting our goals for successful habit formation.

I'm sure we've all tried to set goals for ourselves one way or another. We end every year with New Year's resolutions. Some goals last us a few months, and some don't even survive January. We're so used to failing to reach our goals that at some point we give up on setting them. After all, they don't really work. At the beginning of every year, we get excited about change; we decide we'll "lose X pounds of fat this year and build Y pounds of muscle" or "make Z amount of money." But we don't, and it's depressing.

I'll let you in on a small secret to setting goals that *do* work, and that's what we've been building up to in this book. Most of the goals we choose are based on physical or performance-related achievements. We want to look a certain way, save a certain amount of money, or perform so well at our jobs that we'll inevitably get a promotion. While those are the end results that we want and we can have, we're dealing with the goal-setting process in a completely wrong manner.

We look at goals from the point of view that's all about the rewards we'll get from them. We give very little thought to who we'll become by achieving these goals. And like we've discussed before, something that's against our nature or identity won't stick around for too long. So how about, instead of the goal of losing X pounds a month, we set the goal of becoming a fit person with a healthy lifestyle? Instead of wanting to make X amount of money, how about we decide to become the person who'd make X amount of money?

Setting a goal that focuses on our journey instead of the end result makes all the difference in the world. The wrong approach will keep us struggling, either until we give up on the goal (because it's against our nature) or until we use up every ounce of willpower we have on this goal, discarding everything else in our lives. The right approach focuses on who we'll become as a result of this goal. It builds a constructive framework of habits that we can use to paint the bigger picture, so we grow, one step at a time, in a wholesome manner.

To set identity-based goals, you'll choose an identity that you want to achieve. Next, you'll prove to yourself that you can, indeed, become this person. All it takes is one small win in the direction of the goal, and you'll get to believe you can achieve it. Next, you'll make this identity your central point for building your framework of habits, which will all integrate into a wholesome system—your lifestyle.

The choice of a new identity can be based on several things. You can decide where you want to go and become the kind of person who'd be able to go there, or you can focus on where you're stuck in life and set out to change the current version of yourself. What works best, however, is to build your new identity based on both your vision of who you want to be, and your desire to stop feeling stuck.

Let's look at an example.

Peter is a heavy smoker whose health is falling apart. Smoking is a habit, but it has become his central habit and identity around which his whole lifestyle revolves. Instead of setting a goal to quit smoking as part of his New Year's resolution, he'll set the goal of living a healthy life.

So, his **identity** will be: Someone who has a healthy lifestyle.

And his **small win** will be: Waiting for 30 minutes before lighting the next cigarette during the first day. Once he's able to wait for half an hour, he'll write this achievement down in his journal.

But quitting smoking on its own doesn't result in a healthy lifestyle. He needs to incorporate other habits into his lifestyle, which will help him push toward his new identity. So, he'll set up new, healthy habits, and achieve small wins in every one of them:

Healthy habit #1: Exercise

Small win: Walking for 10 minutes after work

Healthy habit #2: Eating healthy food

Small win: Having a bowl of salad for lunch

184

Healthy habit #3: Getting a good night's sleep

Small win: Sleeping for 8 hours

Healthy habit #4: Meditation

Small win: Starting his day with a 10-minute meditation session

All of these habits might be new, but they all work together toward the new identity that Peter has specified: leading a healthy lifestyle. They also help him overcome the main habit that's ruining his life, which is smoking.

And that's the whole point of goal setting.

You set up an identity that you want to adopt, a lifestyle if you will. Then you identify your worst habits that are keeping you from becoming that person, and your best habits that will, for sure, help you become the best version of that person.

And then, you take it slow. You start by proving to yourself, through small but significant wins, that you are able to make it. You keep taking those steps repeatedly, and you increase them day by day. First, you start by waiting for 30 minutes before smoking the next cigarette, next, you'll wait for an hour. Then two. Then five. Later, you'll only be smoking two cigarettes a day, and then one cigarette every two days. And there you go—your smoking habit has been broken!

By taking these steps slowly but surely, you instill belief and rewire the habits in your brain in the most effective way science has discovered. Before you know it, you'll have developed all the habits you've dreamed of, and overcome the ones that have kept you stuck in place. You'll experience your new identity, enjoying the new life that you've created for yourself from scratch.

You'll be proud.

Your 7-Day Transformation Guide

Your Daily Guide to Becoming a Better Person in Seven Days, Changing Your Life and Achieving Your Goals

We've finally reached the last and perhaps the most important part of this book. This is your daily guide; it's everything you need to do to change your life and achieve your goals—and it all starts with these seven days.

Here are the steps you'll need to take before starting your week of transformation:

1. Choose your new identity.

2. Identify the main habits that are holding you back from this identity.

3. List the habits (behaviors) that will guide you toward your new identity.

4. Specify the small wins over the bad habits you want to overcome, and toward the good habits you want to build

5. Set milestones throughout your journey to measure your success.

6. Set up your habit environment.

7. Start the new routine for seven days—and continue for the rest of your life!

At the beginning of your seven-day journey of transformation, you'll need to have everything planned out in advance. Your new habit loops, the old habit loops and whether you'll replace them or erase them, how these habits work together to create your new identity, and the small wins you'll set out to achieve every day. You'll live every single day of this week in your new identity. Everything you're doing will be about achieving small wins to make you believe in this identity. At the end of the week, you'll know for sure you can make it, because you'll already have done it on a smaller scale.

Transform Your Life with Habits

And now our journey comes to an end.

You started reading this book full of confusion. I know you felt lost and hopeless. You'd tried many times, but every time it ended in failure. It was pretty depressing. But the honest fact is that if we don't understand how our brains and bodies work, we have little chance of making the best out of our lives. If patients try to treat their illnesses themselves, they won't recover. They need to consult a doctor, who will diagnose the condition, explain it to them, and prescribe them the medicine they need to take every day until they get better.

The same goes for our brains. We tend to force ourselves to change our behavior or commit to new ones. We rely on willpower to lose weight, on motivation to go to work, and on self-discipline to resist temptation. And it's only a matter of time before we relapse anyway.

However, changing our lives can be much easier than that. If we learn how to turn the behavior we desire into a habit, we'll go on autopilot. We won't have to think twice before going to the gym, we'll already be on our way. We'll be able to break bad habits like smoking, stress eating, nail biting, procrastination, or any other toxic behavior.

Life transformation through habits starts with the courage to confront the harsh truth. We need to diagnose ourselves first, to pinpoint where we are and how on earth we ended up there. This requires a great deal of self-awareness and brutal honesty. But once we do, once we're fully aware of our deepest desires, we'll know how to make it better. We'll be able to decide whether or not we want to stay where we are, and we'll know exactly where we want to go.

But setting out to achieve our new goals can be tricky. Most of us rely on motivation, which is only an emotional factor. There are days we feel motivated, just like there are days we feel happy, sad, angry, or nothing at all. Risking our success on a turbulent emotion is, well, very risky. Some people know better than that, and if you ask them, they'll tell you the secret lies in your willpower and self-discipline.

Willpower is an amazing feat, but unfortunately, we've learned that we can't depend on it either. You willpower is like a muscle; the more you use it, the stronger it gets. This is great and all, but at the end of the day, it still gets exhausted. It runs out. You can only use it so much, and when you do, you use all of it on one specific goal you're trying to achieve, and end up ignoring other aspects of your life.

The best course of action is to use willpower and self-discipline to your advantage. You'll only be able to do that when you train your brain well enough to go on autopilot to achieve your goals. That's right. You build habits that you wouldn't think twice about, and those habits all come together in a wholesome system that covers the entirety of your new lifestyle.

Our brains create habits in complex, yet simple ways. Habits are the behaviors we perform unconsciously, mostly without even realizing. This trait of automaticity originates from the ability of our brains to form and store these habits for later use. It's all a mechanism that aims to save energy.

The brain creates a habit when you keep repeating the same behavior under the same circumstances. Habit creation consists of four steps: being subjected to an environmental cue, having a craving for what you get out of this habit, performing the behavior itself, and receiving a reward for carrying out the behavior. When you keep all of these circumstances intact, a habit is formed. Your brain then goes on autopilot every time it's subjected to the cue: it starts craving the reward, so it forces you to perform the behavior unconsciously, and then celebrates its reward.

Breaking our habits is difficult because they're deeply ingrained in our brains—but it's not impossible. To change a habit, we need to replace, tweak, or ignore it. But it can't be completely erased. Building new habits is even more difficult. The best way to succeed in this is to exchange pre-existing habits with new, healthier ones.

However, choosing random habits to build will do little good in the grand scheme of things. That's why, instead of making the rash decision to change a single habit or building a new one, it's best to use everything you've learned from this book to create the new lifestyle you want. This new lifestyle will be centered on the new identity you want to assume, and this identity will be your base for setting your goal and changing your habits. But first, you need to believe you can assume this new identity. You need some kind of proof that you're able to build these habits, and that those small steps you're taking will guide you toward your new identity.

You'll choose your new identity based on the version of yourself you want to become. Then, by identifying the bad habits that are keeping you stuck and the good habits that will help build this new version, you'll set up a routine for seven days. On each of these seven days, you'll check your journal for all the small wins you've managed to achieve. Every day, you'll add some more intensity to the steps you're taking.

At the end of your seven-day transformation journey, you'll have become the hero of your own story.